Best of Blue

Best of Blue

Lionel Blue

continuum
LONDON • NEW YORK

Continuum

The Tower Building
11 York Road
London SE1 7NX
UK

80 Maiden Lane
Suite 704
New York, NY 10038
USA

www.continuumbooks.com

First published 2006

British Library Cataloguing-in-Publication Data
A catalogue record for this book is available from the British Library.

ISBN 0–8264–9045–X

Typeset by RefineCatch Limited, Bungay, Suffolk
Printed and bound by MPG Books Ltd, Bodmin, Cornwall

Contents

Contents

Contents

Prologue

At the age of five, I mislaid my soul and was reduced to a body and mind. For some years I didn't even notice any loss, as I didn't believe in the existence of non-sensible realities in any case. In this collection of stories, broadcasts, talks and articles, most out of print and some never in print, I describe my gradual rediscovery of my soul (and how you can recover yours) and how it changed the way I looked at my life and loves, and redefined success and failure. At the universities and colleges I attended I learned to be clever, but that was not enough. I needed something more. Though it was not a 'something' – what was it? – without it I was drying up. Where could I learn compassion, generosity and love? And from whom and how could I learn them? You don't get degrees or doctorates in them.

But I don't want to put on the style. I didn't concern myself with spirituality because it was so beautiful or uplifting, but out of raw need. My adolescent problems were too basic for simple social solutions, and too deep-rooted to grow out of. So I cried 'Help!' just to see what would happen (probably nothing), and something which wasn't 'a thing' happened. It happened in bits, but the biggest bit came during a Quaker meeting in Oxford in November 1951, which I ventured into to get out of the rain. I stayed with spirituality despite my misgivings, and gradually began to trust it because it didn't seem to lead me into cloud cuckoo land but into common sense, as well as some very uncommon sense which I hadn't found in Marx. (It's tragic so much of it went sour under Stalinism.) I also learned a very hard truth, which nonplussed me, that there is no compulsive material evidence in regard to such non-sensible realities as the soul, God, heaven or conscience – just as there is no safe and sure recipe for great art. The only real evidence comes from the devotee himself. In other words, you have to become your own evidence. This is not as bizarre as it sounds. The true worshipper always becomes in part what he or she worships.

At first I enjoyed being on a spiritual high. I mattered in the cosmos, if not in my parents' London suburb. I also chatted to an inner voice so I never felt alone again, which was a plus. I felt loved and wanted. I didn't exactly believe in it, and only began to trust in it when things turned inside out. Instead of me using my soul for cosiness and kicks, it began to use me in ways which contradicted my comforts, plans and pleasures. I found out in a modest way what martyrs and saints and the really righteous had said time and time again, that true religion wasn't just a pussycat but a tiger.

Sometimes I thought I would ditch all this spirituality stuff. But even though I couldn't define what it was, I jolly well knew that when I did so, a part of me dried up. I was in love with it.

Another thing turned inside out too at that Quaker meeting in Oxford. It dawned on me that if the kingdom of heaven was within me, then the sooner I got to know myself honestly, the better. Now, many people want God-discovery without self-discovery because the latter can be upsetting and painful. I found both necessary for each other. For example, I needed the strength that comes from prayer to keep on with the painful probing that analysis requires. Self-knowledge can come in many ways; with me it took the form of analysis.

It was from my analyst that I learned one of the most important lessons of spirituality. He had journeyed to an Ashram in India and after he returned I asked him eagerly if he had found the great guru he was looking for. 'Sort of,' he answered. 'The greatest guru is life itself.' In one way this was helpful. I no longer needed to invest in a robe and begging bowl and join the long line of spiritual backpackers to Nepal. Life, the great guru, lived in north-west London too, so I didn't need to traipse around the Himalayas in fancy dress. But it is very hard to see the extraordinary in the ordinary and the divine in the over-familiar.

As you will learn from the parables and anecdotes in this collection, I discovered truths about life and liturgy on London's Underground Northern Line, and the relation between this life and the Beyond Life while kibitzing a bridge game, and the nature of heaven and hell in hospital waiting rooms. And many other even stranger places, such as saunas and business 'parties', served as my 'unofficial' colleges.

My teachers have been a motley lot and among them were my sceptical mother, my no-nonsense mongrel, some cows, some street people, a gnat and assorted birds such as budgies and doves. I learned a lot from people while watching the arrivals and departures at London stations. There, like Dante, I saw the Human Comedy and the Human Tragedy, and God in them both. It is in human faces that God has become most apparent to me. How this worked out you will read in the following pages.

I had an illumination in the departure lounge when I went on a package holiday. I realized then that this world was a departure lounge, as the rabbis had said. It wasn't my eternal home. So I made myself as comfortable as possible as one does in this world. I made acquaintances. But then I had to leave it willy nilly. In airport chapels I considered how many problems arose from our desire to see this world as our eternal home. But to do this is asking for trouble because it is not that sort of world. It is constantly changing and we are constantly changing with it. I meditated on a line of Talmud. 'Without our consent we are born and without our consent we die and without our consent come before our Creator.' But if it wasn't my eternal home, what was it? Probably a corridor or a school, again as the rabbis had said.

What made my readjustment easier was another 'inside out' I had never expected, but of which you are the beneficiaries as well as me. I had until this time always been heavy in mind and body (I was a comfort eater), suffering periods of worry and depression. The rediscovery of my soul to my surprise made me lighter, almost souffléish. I rediscovered with it laughter I had lost long ago, and the jokes I had learned in my childhood. I began to realize what odd creatures we were.

I began to transmit those jokes and my new exuberance to Jews, gentiles and anyone who was in need of a laugh before they could get out of bed on a cold and miserable Monday morning. They found out, as I had done, that if you do not treat this world as your final home, you can enjoy it much better. Like chocolate in childhood, if you suck it slowly and do not munch it and swallow it quickly, the taste will deepen and become more delicious. But for that you need to trust, to believe.

I listen to arguments about the divine. Is God all-powerful? Is He all-knowing? These do not concern me much. I do not expect Him to produce marvels for me or to make my problems disappear. That would be magic, not religion. I came to God out of need. What I usually need to know from Him is what to do next, to show me the next step ahead and for Him to stick around and give me that little bit of extra courage I need to start doing it. I had learned from Simone Weil that Heaven attracts us with an unseen force like gravity, but once you have spotted it and identified it then you cannot unknow what you do know. That way there is only banality or fanaticism.

But all this will become clearer when you read the life situations and incidents upon which my trust and belief are based. It is much better to feel the proofs which are funny and lively than analyse them. The latter is dreary – we only analyse what was once living but which is now dead.

So open up this book where you like and how you like. Somewhere something in you will respond to something in it. There is a certain pattern in the selection. The chapters begin with childhood and the book ends with the far horizon which comes ever closer. They follow sometimes a time order and sometimes an order of subject, an interest. Enjoy, enjoy!

I dedicate this book to Jim my partner, and my good friends

who redeemed me from an avalanche of paper and who stopped me deleting myself on my own computer, Wendy, Hilary and Julia, Henk and Guy.

Lionel Blue

Dear child

Last Wednesday, when I got home from Birmingham, my mother and my aunt pressed into my hands their birthday presents, for at midnight I would be 56-years-old to me, and 56-years-young to them.

There was some chocolate cake my aunt had baked, a £10 note put aside from their pension and a packet of photos they gave me diffidently because they weren't sure I would want them.

So, to reassure them, I sat beside them on the sofa, munching the chocolate cake, and together we turned over the yellowing pictures.

There was my mother and her sisters in beach pyjamas, strutting out arm in arm, three smart girls who had saved to go to Margate and got there. There was their mother peering nervously into the camera some sunny evening in Stepney long ago. There was my mother again, proud possessor of a dead fox slung around her neck, with limp legs and nasty glass eyes – very 1930s, very smart. And there was my youngest aunt, her sister, fresh and round-faced, lurching along on Louis heels because she wanted to be a femme fatale, though God had designed her otherwise. And then there was me, a child looking speculatively out of the picture, curious as to what kind of life lay beyond the frame.

I hadn't noticed that child for years. I'd never considered him or thought of him. But now I suddenly wanted to speak to him as if there were some unfinished business between us.

So, after my mother and aunt kissed me and went to bed, I sat on, sucking a pencil, laboriously composing a letter just as I used to long ago.

Dear child [I wrote],

I don't know how we are related, if we are, for not one cell of your body lives in mine. I know you tried to imagine me once or twice as you gazed into the future, but you wouldn't recognize me now. I don't know if I've been your friend or foe, for there was a lot of niceness in you I never allowed to grow, but I didn't have much choice!

It is of course your birthday too, and I remember the presents you longed for – a cupcake at the Corner House, meeting a millionaire who would give Dad a job.

I can't even pass on some knowledge which would make your life easier. That sort of knowledge, as you'll learn later, always comes too late, after events not before them.

But as I look at you, your image gazes into me and I see myself without the rucksack of anger and reproaches I've got used to carrying on my back. I wonder what it would be like to let it go. I know from your face that it wasn't always there. Perhaps I can, because as I get older I am closer to being a child again, a second time round, and I become free from grown-up hopes and fears. They say that when people remonstrated with old Golda Meier for smoking, she just said, 'What should happen to me? I should die young!' Well, there are lots of things I've stopped worrying about too – there isn't time.

But her wisecrack has broken my mood and I can't continue this letter – it is too personal. But from it comes this advice for all of you who read it – present or past.

When you try to reconcile yourself to God and to love your neighbours, spare some love for the child who lives within you – whom you haven't thought about for years. He too has a present to give you, though you can give him nothing in return.

A slit of light

After I was born, my mother went into hospital and I was brought up by her mother. The latter was only in her fifties but already very old – a peasant woman to the end of her days. Like her cronies, she was swathed in black shawls, waddling along on rheumaticky legs with slits cut into her shoes to ease her bunions.

In accordance with tradition she wore a sparse wig to hide her female charms, lest her grey wisps inflamed the passions of pious men. Under her wig she hid her savings, two brown ten-shilling notes, fought for penny by penny.

She earned them from casual labour in hotel kitchens where she piped cream over cakes. Sometimes she would risk her job and peep through the swinging service doors at the dancing diners, wondering what life was like if you didn't have to worry about the rent. She stayed there till a chef shooed her away.

The two ten-shilling notes were my inheritance, she never tired of telling me. Her aim in life was to get me out of the ghetto, through those doors, to join the diners from the high life of Highgate and Hampstead.

Well, I've made it as she wished. I write books. One day I might winter in Benidorm and buy a bungalow and I'm grateful granny gave me the shove.

But with the comfort and leisure you buy things granny could not foresee or ever comprehend. Boredom, for example! You need spare time for that and granny never had any. Also the pointlessness of life, once you get what you want. That wasn't granny's problem either. On the wrong side of the service door, there were no senseless suicides, only occasional attempts at murder. Nor was happiness her problem, just survival and respectability. But happiness is a peculiar thing. If you run after it, it runs after you and you never meet. But if you forget it, it just happens. Whether she had it, I don't know, but she never worried about it like me.

Such worry would have bewildered her, but she would have grasped this story of two grannies whose husbands made it and who met on the heights of Highgate.

One said, 'How's life?'

'Fine! Is that your kid in the back of that coupé?'

'Sure.'

'What a nice kid! How old is he?'

'He could walk now,' came the proud answer, 'but thank God, he'll never have to!'

All this ran through my mind as I sat in my dinner-jacket at the top table in a distinguished hotel, about to give an after-dinner speech. I toyed with my glass, then raised a forkful of mille-feuille to my mouth, keeping one eye on the chairman. But my other eye was fixed on a shaft of light in the swinging service door. I could just make out another eye, as black as granny's, staring into the splendour.

I raised my glass to it. It blinked. The swing door swiftly closed, and the slit of light dwindled into darkness.

Streetwise

In 1936, the economic depression lifted and both my parents found work. They left home before seven in the morning and came back, worn out but grateful, after eight, to get me my supper and put me to bed. We no longer had to hide from the rent man.

They paid the grocer, for my tea, and told me to pass the time till they came home, at the play centre or Hebrew classes. I did neither. I discovered the street instead.

As the gasman lit the street lamps, I watched other children through curtain chinks, sitting round their tea tables with their families. I must have felt lonely and resentful, because I remember tying a boy to a lamp-post. He mustn't go home either. He must stay and play with me. I discovered I could be a bully.

I became streetwise quickly. I learned to get into the cinema without paying – slipping past the usherette, changing seats constantly and escaping through the skylight in the gents. I could also wheedle chocolate out of strange grown-ups, by putting on childish charm.

At first, I thought the street was empty, but then I bumped into other children, who also wouldn't or couldn't go home, and roamed the streets like me. They coalesced into gangs who fought like modern nation states. I was allowed into one on probation because of my age and inexperience. But being not quite seven and small had its advantages. It was easier to steal for the gang at Woolworths, while the bigger boys and girls created a diversion.

It all ended in tears. One day my parents came home early to give me a treat. But I wasn't there. I was roving the London docks with my gang.

There was a colossal row, so serious I couldn't comprehend it. Some of the gang were taken into care, but I wasn't a juvenile delinquent, just an infantile one, so I escaped and ended up in religion, not in a reformatory.

Even nice people harbour a criminal inside them. Some call him the evil inclination and some original sin. I remember a charming lady at a party. 'I would murder or steal to help my family get on', she said. Everybody laughed, but I felt uncomfortable. Was it a figure of speech or did she mean it?

When you see gangsters and criminals at the cinema or on TV, it's like looking at animals in the zoo. They're inside the cage and you're outside it. You don't belong to the same species.

But don't fool yourself – you do! Never take respectability for granted, but thank God on your knees for it every day because only an accident or knife-edge separates you from them. I learned that lesson before I was seven. If you haven't learned it yet, you could do a lot of damage and be very dangerous, so take care!

Angels on horseback

What is thy servant but a dog!
(Ancient Semitic inscription)

Come in peace you messengers of peace
Messengers from on high,
From the King above the King of kings
The Holy One – blessed be He!
(Jewish Sabbath hymn to the angels)

Abraham entertaineth three angels
And he lifted up his eyes and looked and, lo, three men stood
by him and when he saw them he ran to meet them . . . and
bowed himself toward the ground.
(Genesis)

Jewish children receive much love, but little protection from the world. All its tragedies and difficulties were discussed in my presence, and while I sat on loving laps I heard no lullabies, but the daily struggles of life instead – politics and unemployment, and the problems of marriage. As a result, I had no time for Snow White or the Sugar-Plum Fairy, and the only story that ever made sense in London's East End was Hans Christian Andersen's *Little Match Girl*. In their place I had something odder but real – the angels – and they have been companions for the rest of my life. I was pleased to help get them back into the liturgy of my synagogue.

As a Jew, I was not used to pictures of religious beings, and my angels had no haloes or wings, and wore no nighties. They were the *mal'achim*, the *angeloi*, the messengers one encountered in one's life who were sent by God. They helped me to cross frontiers, to face what was new, to see the world afresh. Three men met Abraham once: they were significant, they were his angels. Modern Jews get very puritanical about mediators. They want to face infinity directly. I cannot, it is too vast, too dark. I still need angels in my daily life; in prayer I can still talk to them, though it took me years to get over the embarrassment, and I am grateful for their presence, whoever and whatever they are.

The 'angel' who brought me release in my childhood was a Yiddish-speaking horse. She was an ordinary horse and I think her name was Bessie. I do not remember her master's name, but he was a cheerful old Cockney who liked Jews at a time when we needed it and never got very much of it. He taught Bessie Yiddish and, provided it was spoken in a Cockney accent, she understood it. When he shouted '*Shteh*' she stopped, and when he shouted '*Geh*' she began to clip-clop through the East End streets. As she came through Whitechapel I joined a gathering of Jewish schoolchildren and we ran before her, heralding her arrival in excited Hebrew and Yiddish and assorted Slavonic tongues. Many years later, when I heard the gospels read in church, I always mentally put Bessie in the Entry into

Jerusalem. I also imagined her in a sequel – walking slowly and wearily to the knacker's yard, unheralded and unloved.

I suppose her master was really the 'angel', but who can know who is the significant instrument or messenger from beyond?

This Cockney genuinely tried to understand the subtleties of Jewish life. He knew my grandmother never suffered pain but only 'egony', he bravely bit into unfamiliar foods, and lit the fire for us on winter Sabbaths when it was forbidden for us to do so. He understood the anxiety and justified paranoia which ran through Jewish life.

My great-grandparents had been hunted in pogroms. Their children had fled and saved their lives, but they were not saved from their own fears. In the 1930s the streets of London were sharply divided. There were communist streets, and there were fascist streets. There were alleys where no Jewish child could go and others where a good gentile ensured a safe passage (another angel?).

After the Sabbath was out, we used to prepare for our weekly excursion. We could either go to a salt-beef bar in our area; it was Jewish and it was safe, and my aunt might meet suitable young men there, chaperoned by her family. Or away in the West End of London were the Corner Houses, glittering with lights and marble, and with glamorous little orchestras. As I have said, it was not an easy time, for the waves of fear and terror were returning as the first refugees arrived from Germany with tales of shame and humiliation. Should we stay among ourselves or venture beyond Aldgate Pump into 'real' England? We needed reassurance. Sometimes we heard the Yiddish horse in the distance and it gave us, I think, that little extra courage we needed to meet gentiles.

In my life I have met other angels, and an unlikely lot they are. An angel can be the first person you fall in love with, who lets you down gently and lightly and helps you go forward into the risks of light and love. You can hear one in a bus queue whose name you will never know but who says something which answers some inner questions, some need which is barely understood. It can be that intimate and strange figure, one's guardian angel. The analyst who came to my aid at a party was a messenger to me of deep significance. So was a charwoman, so was a Carmelite nun I only saw behind a grille. So was an East End horse. Understanding one's own, defending one's own and loving one's own are natural. Through a few creatures, human or animal, we are redeemed from our limitations and learn to meet what is strange and unfamiliar, and this is not quite natural – it is a little more, therefore it is supernatural. It is the only other religious lesson that has stayed with me from that period.

I stress that all this is real for me still, though such beliefs are not in fashion either in the religious or in the secular world in which I move. If it helps anyone, I willingly accept the mythical quality of my angels, though they are mostly very solid. The acceptance of them has meant that the incidents of my life are not accidents for me; they are clues to a meaning I sometimes grasp but cannot keep. These clues do not just form inside me, they are waiting there for me in external reality – if I can reach them.

Events in themselves are not this meaning; they are just the clues to it. Like words, they have to be read. When I later became a rabbi and people came to see me, I believed their words at first. I did not read through them because I did not know how to. Soon I realized that what they said pointed to something deeper. This is so in conversation, in reading the Scriptures, and through events. I realized this as a child when I met my angel, and I am coming to realize it again. I did not realize it so well in my teens and twenties.

Becoming a man

The Bar Mitzvah party was drawing to its close. Saturated with piety and pastries, the guests were thanking their hosts and making late farewells. The confirmation had gone off well, and everything that was supposed to be said in the speeches had been said.

The boy had read from the scroll in the synagogue without a single mistake, or so his father said. I had spotted three but kept quiet about it.

The rabbi had urged him to be a modern Maccabee and fight the good fight. His father had exhorted him to play the game – and he didn't mean poker, ha ha! – and marry a girl with a heart as big as his mother's, which was impossible, of course. The guests had chorused 'hear, hear!'. The boy had committed himself, rather recklessly I thought, to a life of unlimited virtue, to abstain from pork and other impurities not to be mentioned. He promised to marry a nice Jewish girl who would love his mother as she deserved, which was impossible, of course.

Exhausted by so many prayers and promises, the Bar Mitzvah boy and I stared at each other over the debris on the table.

'What loot did you get?' I asked.

'Four fountain pens, seven ties, three watches and a video. What did you get at yours?'

'A gas mask case, four savings stamps, three clothing coupons and half a packet of dried egg – there was a war on.'

'It couldn't have been much of a party', he commented.

'It was fabulous', I said. 'My father went to Epstein and commissioned him to model my head in chopped egg and onions for the top table.'

'And did he?' asked the boy, round-eyed.

'No', I said and shook my head sadly. 'He said now he only worked in mashed baked beans because there was a war on and my father should try Picasso or Henry Moore instead.'

'Oh, you're just another joker', said the boy. 'I wish some-one would give me some straight answers sometimes', he added, exasperated.

I thought back to my own Bar Mitzvah and all the questions I hadn't dared to ask. 'Go ahead', I said. 'I'll answer straight.'

'Well, do you believe all the stuff you read from the prayer book?' he said.

'No,' I said, 'I can't.'

He looked startled. 'Doesn't that worry you?'

'It used to,' I admitted, 'but not now. The prayer book states what our forefathers believed – yours and mine – but my life has been different from theirs. I've had experiences they never had, and if I try to believe exactly the way they did, it wouldn't work. It would feel as strange as wearing their clothes. But when I recite the prayers, I'm loyal. I add my own faith to theirs, and their prayers continue through mine.'

This was a new thought and he asked, 'But you do practise what you preach, don't you?'

'Not even that', I said gently. 'I try to, like you, but I fall down, say sorry, pick myself up and fall down again. I don't stop trying though. That's why I'm religious. Perfect people don't need religion.'

'It's so complicated', the boy said fretfully.

'Yes,' I said, 'but you're a man now and you have to cope with the complications. The truth makes you free – it doesn't make you cosy.'

'Is that from Scripture?' he said.

'Yes,' I said, 'but not ours, though the rabbis said the same sort of thing. That's another complication.'

He got up and said good night politely. He had stepped into grown-up religion, and wasn't sure if he liked it.

'It'

As a boy I was eager to learn but ignorant – and my parents, teachers and rabbis, who were usually so generous with advice and information, on this subject gave nothing away. I turned therefore to other sources. I read Leviticus, and learned all that I should not do (incest and women's clothes) but not what I should do, and how I should do it. The radio was more helpful. 'Birds do it', sang the lady, and I listened intently. 'Bees do it – even educated fleas do it.' I turned this last piece of information over in my mind. It was a curious piece of the jigsaw, but as yet I could not determine its position or its relevance, so I listened to the lady once more. 'Let's do it', she crooned, 'Let's do it again.' Again! Puberty was on the horizon, and I was prepared to do it even if only once and die for ever – if I ever learned how to, of course.

Did adults do it? The evidence pointed that way, but common sense revolted. If adults did it, then my parents must do it, which seemed unlikely, and my rabbi must do it, which seemed incredible. How could he do it? Would he wear his black gown or just his linen tabs, and surely he would have to keep his velvet hat on. Would he moan in English, Yiddish or Hebrew? This was exotic stuff. It was so absurd that I turned back to the birds, the bees and the educated fleas.

I have been 20 years in the ministry, and religion has never lost this coyness. Four-letter words are respectable enough for the Oxford Dictionary but they can never make the pulpit, though my congregations, like everybody else, are doing it – and after doing it, do it again. This I know as their minister.

This coyness can be charming, but it is dangerous when religion and reality part company. Ordinary people have become more honest, and religious establishments have to catch up. Evasion is not purity, and the facts of life were not, after all, thought up by a dirty old man, but by divinity itself. I have, for example, seen three great changes in the last 20 years concerning 'it' which have scarcely been acknowledged in seminaries, even my own.

Sex has been separating itself from procreation and now often wears no fig leaf of biological purpose. It has therefore to be considered as pleasure, and religion is not good with pleasure. Traditionally, religion has used poverty and deprivation to provide the power for spiritual ascent. Yet sex and spirituality need each other. To accept the sexual needs of another person (emotional, physical and technical) requires a listening as profound as that required by prayer. Religious people preach and teach many lessons to the secular world. This is a lesson they have to learn from it.

A second change has affected the roles of the sexes. They are no longer fixed, and couples work out their own balance of functions and duties. This concerns washing up, cooking, sexual positions, and is beginning to affect ritual as well. A man can do the washing up, and a woman does not always have to look up at the ceiling. There is more muddle but there is also more experiment, more understanding and more generosity.

A third change concerns the needs of sexual minorities which have scarcely been acknowledged, let alone understood. This has been a serious defect in the system, for the number is constant and their contribution to religion has been significant, if unacknowledged. Unfortunately they have been considered 'outsiders' – so those who need spirituality for their relation-ships (they have few social props) are precisely those who have been turned away from it.

I was heartened, though, by an article in the newspaper. One rabbi – the first in this country – had defied all precedent and come out with 'it', so to speak. If only this had happened in my childhood, all doubts would have been set at rest. Seven months' pregnant in a maternity gown – a rabbi conducted a service. Truth was at last visible and I rejoiced.

I hasten to add, the rabbi was a woman.

A starker Spain

After the war, when school ended I used to hitch south. At the Med, I always turned left to Provence, never right to Spain, because that country held bad memories for me, though I'd never been there. Two of my cousins – the heroes of my childhood – had died fighting Fascism in the Civil War. I'm grateful to package holidays which finally got me across that frontier, because they have abolished the horrors of history. The look-alike hotels have no past, just as their poolside romances have no future. Each wave of new tourists wipes away all traces of the one before.

But on the Costa Blanca, around the anniversary of my cousins' death, someone said there was a Civil War memorial in nearby Alicante and reluctantly I had to remember them. When I asked a tourist office how to get there, they tried to fob me off. Wouldn't I prefer a mock medieval banquet with chicken and chips? Yes, of course, but 'No, I wouldn't!' So, after a lot of telephoning around, they grudgingly gave me a train number and the name of a stop.

In Alicante, I fortified myself at the bright new burger bar, and then found the tram. It clanked past bright tourists' bars, then past solid serious banks – then along a long dusty road, lined with old lorries, to a starker Spain, without bright lights, that was tourist-free. When I enquired haltingly, 'Guerra Civil?' one old man nodded and led me to the door of a youth hostel where he shook my hand.

Along a corridor behind another door was the saddest prison I'd ever seen, unaltered since the Civil War. Each grey cell contained one table, one tin plate and a straw mattress on a stone floor. They looked onto a gaunt chapel.

I sat by an old woman – the only worshipper – and as she prayed for the fallen heroes, I thought of my cousins and responded 'Amen' – 'So may it be!' I followed her into the yard, and bowed my head as she laid red paper flowers by a plaque marking the execution-place. Perhaps my cousins had died here. Then I read the plaque and froze. I had prayed for the wrong martyrs, the ones my cousins had given their lives against. I suddenly remembered with tears how a great-aunt's hair had turned white when she heard the news of their death.

But can you unpray prayers? It seemed both wrong and ridiculous to carry on the Spanish Civil War into the afterlife and eternity. Worn down by conflicting feelings, I reluctantly responded 'Amen' again. The Spanish Civil War, which ended in 1938, had finally died in me. Bless them all, bless them all, I thought wearily, the long, the short, the tall, the lot!

May God bind them all into the gathering of life.

Making it big in the next life

I stood outside a pie shop frowning and waiting to be interviewed for an outside broadcast on London market life. Something deep down was bugging my memory, but what?

Yes, I certainly remembered trying to make a pie myself once. I mixed the dough according to the instructions, and tried to roll it out with a milk bottle, which drove me frantic for it kept shredding into lace. I tried to repair the holes by gluing them first with water and then with spittle, until the pastry got as grey as I felt. And in a burst of temper, I threw the grisly lump through the window, where it hit my dog, who howled. The recipe never told me about flouring the pastry board. Now, there was no beautiful thought in that.

And then I still sometimes indulge in a childhood fantasy of being locked up in a pie shop overnight. I'd nibble a bit of crust here and try a filling there, till I collapsed, gorged but happy, to greet the dawn with a bump, which is not a very beautiful thought either.

And then it hit me. A pie shop in a market, that's where my father taught me the facts of life, or tried to, for I was only five at the time. This is how it happened.

In the Great Depression my family fell on hard times. My

father was an out-of-work master tailor. He and my mother tried their hand at a sweet shop, but father was no businessman and he was far too generous. He gave away most of the stock, and my mother ate the rest. Which is how he came to be in an east London market, selling ice cream in the depths of winter. He sat me in a nearby jellied eel and pie shop. It was warm and through the window he kept an eye on me, while I kept two fascinated eyes on two mangy dogs, one of whom was mounting the other.

Now I hand it to my father, he didn't dodge the issue – unlike the nanny of an upper-class friend of mine. When he was faced with the same sight, she told him one poor doggy was ill, dear, and the other was a doggy VAD nurse, who was wheeling it to hospital. This would have certainly sounded more plausible than the things my embarrassed father tried to tell me, which I thought more fanciful than any fairy story and far more horrible.

Suddenly he stared at the two exhausted dogs, stopped and bolted out of the shop. He returned with one decrepit pooch, covered with suppurating sores. My father demanded a pail of water, carbolic soap and disinfectant, which he got because he was a big man and a boxer. Then to the consternation of the management and undeterred by the cries and complaints of the customers, whose appetites he was spoiling, he washed the dog in the doorway all over, fondling it and feeding it his own jellied eels.

I cringed with embarrassment and tried to apologize for him. But then a beefy market man, who was one of the loudest complainers, turned to me and said, 'Don't apologize for your dad, boy! He makes us mad, but you might not know it, he's a saint!'

Which shut me up sharply! Even if my father turned out to be no tycoon in this world, he might make it big in the next. He certainly failed to teach me the facts of life. I found out those later by trial and error, with more of the latter than the former, alas. But I did learn what goodness is like, which is a fact of eternal life. It was a fair swap.

Anyway, that's what bugged my memory as I stood frowning while I waited by a pie shop in a market.

Dutch courage

In Dutch cities, religion has to take its place among all the other passions of people. Apart from a few show pieces, the churches are set among the ordinary houses in the street, between cafés, bookshops and shops selling anything from sex to souvenirs. And yet I learned something there which I never found in London – and it wasn't sex or souvenirs, it was just simplicity of speech, or honesty. I didn't even find it in a seminary or a synagogue or a church, but in the devastating directness of Dutch daily life. You can find truth in holy places, but commonplace honesty is a rarer bird.

I went to Holland just after the war. My school had advertised a holiday there, where we children could view lots of cows and clogs in clean air, and be respectful over the Rembrandts.

The holiday never took place because of an understandable lack of enthusiasm among the children. We had all had enough clean air in the country during our evacuation, and what we wanted was city dirt and dust and dance halls where we could wear our new ties from America. They had girls painted on them and, if you were lucky, would light up with the help of a battery in your breast pocket.

The school regretfully notified my parents that the holiday

was off, but I intercepted the note, said polite farewells, and that is how I arrived in Rotterdam, marvelling at my freedom, but not sure what to do with it.

I was rescued by a Dutch family who gave me my first lesson in false politeness, or fibs. There was a plate of cream cakes on their table, a treat I hadn't had for years.

'Have one, Lionel', they said. 'Oh, I really couldn't', I said primly, perfidiously licking my lips. (My parents had told me never to accept at once. You took one after two refusals.) And then to my indignation the plate was passed on to the other end of the table. They didn't seem to know their lines. They should have responded, 'But Lionel, you must have one.' I would then say, 'But really this is too much!' They would then add, 'But, please', and I would answer, 'Well, a small one, then', and take the biggest off the plate.

The look of that cream cake has never left me. I can still recall its creamy, fruity juiciness, for in memory it is mine. I still think of it whenever I am tempted to part from the truth. If I put on the style in a pulpit, for example, and pretend to believe more than I do, or say more saintly sayings than I have a right to, then that piece of pastry is an awful warning against pretence, whether for the sake of piety or politeness.

Another shock came at a dinner party. The gentleman sitting next to me said quite simply, 'I don't like you very much.' Emboldened by the bracing Dutch air, I answered equally simply, 'I don't like you either.' After that we chatted amiably, and when we meet after all these years we still greet each other reasonably, though without rapture.

In England, the dreadful thing is that the more people dislike you, the more polite they are, which is very confusing if you aren't quite English. They have a clever combination of unpleasantness and politeness no continental can match.

Anyway, that is why I suddenly bought a cheap excursion-ticket to Holland and set off rejoicing from Liverpool Street Station.

When I got to Amsterdam, the cafés were almost collapsing with the energy of their clientele, who were bellowing the fast waltzes of the place. Everybody was telling everyone else exactly what they thought of them, and I did too. Instead of trying to love mankind, I decided instead to be straight with my neighbour. It's harder than you think!

A dream of marble halls

The most memorable holiday I ever had was also the cheapest and the earliest. The brochure said I could have five or six nights and four days (or was it the other way round? I lost count of the nights and days – I was too confused) for about a tenner – everything thrown in. It was long, long ago! I have always had a weakness for bargains and I needed a break, so I signed on and joined the jolly package.

We were sent off in the early hours of the morning when the departure lounge lived up to its name and seemed reserved for the dear departed. It looked ghostly and we looked ghastly. I knew it would take me five or six days and four nights (or vice versa) to recover – and then, my God, I thought, it would all begin again. For the first time in my life I wrung my hands.

We arrived at our hotel in the early hours and its unexpected grandeur muddled me more than ever. The foyer was filled with marble and the chandeliers were like those in Lyons Corner Houses before the war. It was stupefying and I wondered if I had wandered onto a film set. There was even more marble in my room – so much marble that it reminded me of that superior suburban cemetery where I shall eventually lodge as a long-term guest (a synagogue kindly gave me free burial rights as a parting gift – it was well meant).

Before I tried to sleep I examined the furniture and had another surprise – it was concreted in! Surely clientele who were fit for such marble halls would not nick the commodes. Such low suspicions in such high living didn't fit.

There was a lot that didn't fit, in fact. Just as I dozed off, an institutional bell clanged along the classy corridors. Blearily, I went down to breakfast and in a dream ate sugared buns under crystal chandeliers at a table with two elderly ladies and one drunk.

The ladies said the weather wasn't what they had expected in the south. I said politely it would be more bloody in the north, and the drunk reproved me in a hoarse whisper for using foul language in front of the fair sex. He told me to mind my 'q's and 'p's. 'P's and 'q's, I corrected absent-mindedly, and ill-advisedly. An explosion was averted by an announcement. Shortly after breakfast we would be welcome in the local nightclub, whose management would treat us to one free glass of 'champagne' each. The ladies gasped. They had never been near a nightclub, nor had I, at noon.

In the club itself some grey light glimmered through the cracks onto the purple poufs and scarlet tables. I sipped the sweet froth and decided I had fallen down a rabbit hole and would make the best of it.

The only other hole open in town, where we could also make the best of it, was a liqueur shop (not a liquor shop). It sold every liqueur imaginable and some which weren't. At 11 am you could freak out on sweet alcohol, flavoured with banana, quince, quinine or gold-leaf. Some looked like perfume and some just tasted like it. The weather was appalling and the town deserted. We looked at each other and had another one for the road – though if I remember rightly, none of the roads there were complete.

When we got back to the hotel we were told to tone up for a pageant of local dance. Then we would visit a shrine, and then we would begin some bingo. Never was so much experienced by so few for so little.

Since that package so many years ago, my admiration for the value provided by our tourist industry for the British holiday-maker has never wavered. The latter didn't want to let the side (what side?) down. So they queued for their morning bubbly, and prayed at the shrine, and pretended to be partial to fancy dress and sugared buns instead of rashers, and when they were holed up in the hotel by a gale they sang 'Lily of Laguna' and 'We'll hang out the washing on the Siegfried Line' – which startled a German group who were being loaded in just as we were packed out.

Since those far-off days, costs have become keener on the costas and you don't get much marble now for a tenner, if any But the breakfast buns still carry the same quota of sugar. I can't remember where I went. Come to think of it, I never really knew.

Pig and Jew

At university I studied the humanities, but humanity itself I learned on a crowded train. I recognized the Yugoslav station when it suddenly flashed on my TV screen, though just after the Second World War, it wasn't much of a station – only two huts. One housed a machine gun, and the other, with two doors, the conveniences. We foreigners couldn't read the Slav inscriptions, so the men galloped through one door, and the women through the other, and we all collided at one unisex hole.

The train was equally makeshift but alive. Bodies swung from racks, strangers took turns on each other's knees, and peeped between your legs. There were Serbs, Croats, Bosnians and Slovenes, though you had to be one to know which was which. A former Nazi youth was making his way to Moscow and two Albanians toasted the British Communist leader, Harry Pollitt, as 'our little red flower'.

A sobbing girl had lost her luggage, and the other passengers out of their nothing contributed a tattered scarf and a slice of grilled goat.

As our train hiccoughed across Yugoslavia, we exchanged pointed Eastern European proverbs and stories. I bridled when one genial gent informed us that Galicians and Bessarabians would both sell you their grandmother, but only the Galicians would deliver. My grandpa's family came from Galicia.

'OK, tell us your story', he says soothingly.

'An anti-Semite,' I say meaningfully, 'tells a Jew on a train, "In the town we just passed, you can't find a pig or a Jew." "What a pity," says the Jew, "we didn't get off there together." ' An old peasant woman suddenly laments that no one has enough pig any more, and we all laugh. The German lad exclaims joyously how wonderful it is, for only 40 months earlier we were all killing each other, Serbs, Croats, British, Germans and Jews – which is tactless but true. In the silence that follows, I ponder our tribalism, which is what nationalism really is, and what a blasphemous business it is. The religious greats warned against it.

Paul said, 'In Christ there is neither Jew nor Greek', and the Hebrew prophets, 'Hath not one father created us?' And the last words of a Hindu soldier, as he was pierced by a British bayonet, were, 'And you are also divine'.

I left the train near the Serbo Croat boarder. They fondled and kissed me and we swore *bratstvo* – eternal brotherhood. Later, back home, I was taught Englishness at university and Jewishness at my seminary. But on that train they taught me to be a human being. It's tragic that the killing started up again there, for they were the salt of the earth. It's such a tempting trap – loving your own more at the price of loving others less. Unfortunately that's what modern nationalism means, and it leads to hell.

Bus stop

I bumped into him by the bus stop outside the psychiatric hospital. He looked lost, as patients do after their discharge. He could go home now – if he had one, which he hadn't, because his wife had had enough and left him. I pieced his story together while we waited.

We were going the same way, so we stopped off at a café, and celebrated his release with beans, bangers and doughnuts. But how was he going to get started in an empty flat, when there was nothing to wake up for?

'Join the club', I said. 'Lots of people can't get started. Some can't fill in a form. Some can't post a letter. Some can't cope with the washing up and have to eat out.'

In my teens and early twenties I couldn't get out of bed. I lay there listening to the letters sliding through the letter box and the ringing phone. It wasn't laziness, but fear. They were demands which turned into threats as I delayed.

'Now comes the padre's pep talk on the power of prayer', he said caustically – he was entitled to his feelings. 'Prayer didn't save me,' I said, 'it was the BBC light programme. If I turned it on when I woke up, my world wasn't empty. If I managed to move my body to the rock 'n' roll beat, it shifted my mood too.

I used to hokey-cokey round the bedroom and shimmy and shake to the bathroom.'

'Crikey!' he said, and I admit a naked trainee rabbi on a rug, cutting a rug, is not a pretty sight, but who cares if you're on your own?

'Give me some more tips', he said, beginning to enjoy himself. 'Well, I sang. Not hymns, but rugger songs, advertising jingles and Rosenkavalier – all parts. And if I could get down and dressed, I rewarded myself with a tin of cold custard.'

'So God didn't come into it?' he said sardonically, for like many people he was a spiritual snob who couldn't see God in ordinary things like cold custard, only in extraordinary sensational ones.

But religion doesn't need an 'r' in the month, so I told him the story of the rabbi who was marooned in a flood on the roof of his synagogue.

First a lifesaver swam towards him, but passed him by because the rabbi gave no signal, for God would find him in His own time. Then a lifeboat also passed by, but the rabbi meditated on in silence. The flood waters rose higher, and then the rabbi prayed. 'I wait patiently for your salvation, Lord, how long?' A voice came from heaven. 'I've already sent my salvation twice, you blithering idiot, and you sent it back both times.'

'God redeemed me via the radio, the hokey-cokey and tins of cold custard. Have another doughnut.'

He laughed. 'Will God come to me too?' 'But he already has,' I said, 'and you haven't noticed it – just like the rabbi in the story. God has already used me to make you laugh again.' He was puzzling over this theological conundrum when we parted. For the first time he had forgotten his sorrows.

Home from home

In 1940 an invasion was expected hourly. My parents brought me back to London from the country, and each night we slept in the vaults of a brewery in the Mile End Road. After the morning all-clear, we packed up our bedding, and hurried back home to see if we still had one.

One day it wasn't there – just a smoking hole instead. My mother found a barrow and my father loaded onto it the remnants, a bakelite Ekco radio with its bottom blown off and a dud shell I'd collected that Dad turned into a cigarette lighter. My father then wheeled the barrow to the lockup for bombed-out people like us, and that was that.

I never quite trusted 'real' things after that. And this distrust is confirmed as I drop into charity shops on my way to work, and sift through the debris of other people's hopes and homes.

During a wandering life, I've learned how to make my home in hotels, hospitals, boarding houses and bed-sits instead. It's useful knowledge and I'll tell you how it's done, because you may have reserved a room in a high-rise hotel for your holiday this summer on some crowded costa. It sounded beautiful in the brochure but when you let yourself into it, it's so blank and bright and un-homey you want to rush out to the nearest bar or bistro to find something familiar and friendly.

Well, why not make friends with the room first! Don't unpack, just potter. Pretend you're an artist and consider its light and shade and shadows. Don't turn on the radio, risk the room's silence. Sit still in it, let the silence surround you, and suck you into itself. But you're worried whether the tap will drip, or the blind will get stuck. The only thing worth worrying about is worrying. You can't complain to the management just because your room's pleasant, not perfect.

Instead, make friends with yourself as well as the room, because home is in you, not just your hotel. The walls you resent are only mirrors reflecting back your own restlessness. Let the silence of your room swallow up your faults and failures and its emptiness purify you.

Now it's time to make friends with God. And this is how you do it. Relax, open your hands and lay them palm upwards on your knees and ask God in to be your guest. When His still small voice starts to sing in the silence, close your eyes. When they open in their own time, your blank, bright room will seem more kind and cosy.

Now you're ready to saunter down for a drink in the hotel bar, confident because you've got a home to return to, not just a room. And you may remember some old familiar words as you sip your sangria, 'And God saw all He had created and behold, it was very good.'

Granny's juju

The Holocaust was commemorated for a day, but it altered my religion for ever. When I was five, my granny said if I prayed for something unselfish, God would make it happen. So I prayed for Hitler to drop dead, but he didn't. Granny's pious juju hadn't worked, so I marched with the reds instead.

I did so until the late 1940s but I hadn't enough faith for Stalinism. So I left the march, which was still chanting inanely the names of his East European mafia, and celebrated my defection with a curry. Not long after that I fell into a Quaker meeting by chance and became cautiously religious.

But I hadn't been a materialist for 15 years for nothing, and I'm still not into miracles whatever their provenance, except the wonder of experiencing heaven in the here and now.

I know some good people do expect happenings and they'd like me to teach them some prayer to make their problems vanish, to alter the universe to suit their situation. I sympathize, but I can't do that even for myself, let alone for them.

The Holocaust stops me because I can't help thinking of all the prayers, some of the sincerest ever, said in those cattle trucks on the way to the extermination camps, most of which were never answered in any way we can understand.

So why have I started to pray again? Because I've discovered that though prayer doesn't change the cosmos, it changes me. It doesn't make my problems vanish but it gives me enough courage to face them, and that's the difference between magic and religion. And when I face them, I sometimes glimpse a light shining in darkness.

But I must keep my feet on the ground. Practically speaking, prayer shows me what I have to do next in life and it gives me some extra strength to do it. Like many people, I used to feel nausea at the sight of blood. But I still had to do my hospital visiting. When I entered, I just prayed 'Help!' and got enough strength to finish my work. When the nausea came back, I rewarded myself with coffee and custard pie. Another instance! If I ask God before a meeting to be present to me at a conference, service or theatre, I think less about myself, more about the people I'm talking to and the difference shows.

Two men were boasting about their rabbis. One man said 'Our rabbi performs miracles. His prayers are so poignant, even God is moved to do his will. He can't help himself.'

The other chap replies, 'Our rabbi performs miracles too. His prayers are so powerful that occasionally he even rushes to do God's will – he can't help himself, he says.'

The first I know nothing about. The second one could be me.

Chow

It's after midnight – I can't sleep, so I twiddle my transistor and tune in to a religious talk. I hear the same advice I've so often given others (you perhaps). Get up, get out and do good deeds! But as I'm fastened to a drip and pacemaker, I can't do any deeds, good or otherwise – I can only be done to.

If you're bedridden and feeling useless and frustrated – I recommend to you a curious scripture, neither Jewish nor Christian but Chinese, that helped me.

I came by it when I was up at Oxford in the 1950s. The Church of England was as bothered by the South India question then as it is by lady bishops and civil partnerships now. I was fascinated by religious rows, and sat absorbed in chilly church halls, sucking sweets. There I met a Chinese student, equally absorbed, who I called Chow – though whether Chow was his Christian name, surname, or what he ate, I never knew. He was a sweet, silent chap, whose only outburst occurred in a café. An advert said if you wanted to look special, you should use a certain cigarette holder. All the students there were looking special, and sucking the same cigarette holders. Chow became hysterical and couldn't stop cackling.

He vanished from Oxford quietly, leaving a translation of

that curious Chinese scripture in my pigeon hole with no note. No one even knows its author's name (I don't know Chow's either) – only his nickname 'Old Boy' – Laó Tse in Chinese.

Look at your window, says the Old Boy. The important part isn't the frame, but the hole which lets in the light. Gaze into your teacup! The useful part isn't the container but the hollow it contains. It's the things you don't do, the empty times, which give your life value.

Strange advice, which doesn't just apply to invalids. You go to a prestige party. You want to shine and think of a beautiful bitchy remark. God bless you if you don't say it, and let the others think you are dull.

You're racing your trolley round the supermarket trying to find the fast check-out. Take the first fate provides, and don't export your tension!

You're stuck in a hospital bed. Before you summon the night nurse, relax into your weakness. See if the harmony of heaven works through you!

Some people you don't expect understand this message instinctively. At Sunday School the clever kids were shouting 'Sir, Sir', and waving their hands to get my attention. One very clever girl didn't because she thought the unclever ones should have a chance. You have to be very big to be a nobody!

Now, all my life I've tried to be a somebody. But in the hospital ward I let go. I was a nobody, I knew it, at one with the snuffles from the beds nearby, the whispers of the nurses and the moonlight tumbling through the window. A burden had gone, just as Old Boy said. I stopped twiddling and fell asleep like a child.

Guardian angel at Gatwick

In Gatwick airport, beyond the departure desk, lies Gatwick Village with its hamburger hostelry and chapelette with interfaith furnishings.

I sidled in because my flight was late, but sat up during the sermon. 'Did we know,' the preacher said, 'that each plane carried twice the number of passengers that had checked in?' No, I didn't and didn't want to!

He continued. 'Invisible presences without boarding passes come with us. They are our guardian angels.'

I relaxed and laughed. My guardian angel! I hadn't thought of him since the Blitz – when he made me sleep more securely.

Amused, I invoked his presence. He could come with me to Rome, where he could meet lots of other angels, adult ones taking off from towers, or blowing trumpets on marble tombs, and fat baby ones adjusting their diapers on frescoes.

Now I don't know who angels are, what they are, or whether they are, but their presence does make a difference.

While I was with a group down in the catacombs, we saw something small and alive twittering beside a tomb. Someone said soothingly, 'It's only a bat'. So, relieved of responsibility, we groped our way through the graves to the exit.

'You know it isn't a bat,' said my guardian angel, 'but a bird that's fallen through the roof. If you don't go back, I don't know how you'll ever have the face to give that nice sermon again, about caring for God's creatures.'

Well, neither did I – and there was a lot of wear still in that sermon. Sulkily I left the group, got the bird, and in the dark I took the wrong turning. When they finally found me, I was as shaken as the fluttering feathers in my hand.

'Come on, let's visit those deluxe shops on the Via Condotti', said my guardian angel soothingly. 'You like all that Gucci Pucci stuff.' 'But I can't afford those things.' 'You can enjoy without owning', said my guardian angel. 'Any angel can teach you that.'

Well, we had a wonderful time window shopping and a polite assistant gave us free squirts of aftershave.

Later on in Santa Maria, we sat companionably together, examining the golden angels in the mosaics. 'Stay with me', I said. 'Where do we go next together? Los Angeles?' he said hopefully. I laughed. Well, I would certainly need a guardian angel there.

Now, I don't know whether my guardian angel is fact or phantasy – whether he's a religious reality or something cooked up in my psyche. But do take your own guardian angel along with you on holiday. Whether he'll guard you against pick-pockets and muggers, I don't know. But he'll certainly guard you against your own worst enemy – yourself.

The God cage

As I was driving down the road with an Irish friend, we passed a church with a modern bell-tower. At the top was a belfry made of iron bars. 'By God', said my friend. 'Sure, they've done it at last! 'Tis what they've always wanted. They've caged the Almighty.' He brooded a moment and then shook his fist at the offending structure and shouted: 'But He won't endure it. He'll never let them get away with it. He'll get even with the boyos yet . . .', etc., etc.

Now institutional religion (I call it 'Religion with a big R') is like a box. If you like the idea of a religious box, then you call the box a shrine or a reliquary – if you don't, you call it a God-cage. When I decided to study for the rabbinate, I liked the idea of living with others in a religious box. Inside we might be droopy, but we would at least be pure. It would provide a foretaste of the communion of saints and the life of the world to come. But I found a seminary wasn't a box, it was more like a boxing ring, a mirror reflecting all life, sacred and profane, in it.

Because I was an adolescent with pimples, I got disillusioned and decided to leave religion and go to hell in my own way. I would be a devil, I thought, and say 'No' to God and 'Yes' to anything anybody should ever ask me, if they asked me, which was more than I dared hope.

And that period of my life was quite exciting, because I met people who cohabited, lived together and paired off in quite extraordinary combinations and sequences. My puzzle was that they didn't seem to get much pleasure out of it. I listened as they anguished, analysed and agonized over their interesting state. 'Well,' I thought, 'a Jewish suburban marriage should be like a rest cure after this!'

For though my new friends thought they lived outside God, I knew God lived inside them. I saw His fingerprints on their lives. Though they thought they were the great unblessed without any benefit of clergy, their lives glittered with undisciplined acts of generosity and love, in fact they continued my religious education, teaching me the same truths as my seminary, but with different illustrations.

I learned again that God is everywhere. He resides in Arks and on altars, as any worshipper knows through experience. But if you seek Him, you find Him, in boardrooms and bed-rooms, in hymns ancient or in juke-box modern, in discos or pubs. In God, distinctions between rich and poor, slave and free, Jew and Greek, or German or Arab for that matter, don't matter. You can learn this from the spirituality of Paul, or it can be deduced from the lowest common denominator of human experience – a shared hangover.

I learned that God is my eternal home – He is not my life sentence in jail. So why do we try to limit God? It is because He is so vast, and the distance that separates us so daunting. We get tired of straining upwards so that He can reach us. We cop out and try to make Him smaller and lower, so that we can reach Him — a deity just the right height for a cage or a kennel. But the world shows us how foolish that is. My liturgy asks a great question: 'Where is the place of God's glory?' I understood afresh the answer: 'Blessed is the Lord, whose glory is revealed in every place!'

Take care – take care!

Life's a tricky old thing, and getting trickier all the time. There is a substitute for everything now, and the picture on the package tells you more about you and what you want to believe than the contents. You can be a martyr, for example, without discomfort, or a revolutionary just for the kicks, or you can disguise your private hates with social concern.

You can imitate the Spirit too. With practice you can fool people with your imitation of it. You can even fool yourself if that's what you want. But you won't fool the Spirit. That dove is a wise old bird, with that knowing look you find in untamed creatures.

Take gentleness, for example. There has been an awful lot of it around since the hippies moved in from California, and flower-power people pressed dying daisies into your hand in Oxford Street. The kindness was clinging, but sticky like chewing gum, and you couldn't get away from it. Even in pubs your own mates didn't give you a hearty farewell. They looked into your eyes, the rats, sadly and soulfully, and gently said, 'Bless you, take care!' on a rising note.

Now you can be gentle but not because the Spirit moves you, but because you are so bloody feeble you can't be anything else. It's easier to agree with everybody, even if they are wrong, than to disagree with them because you are right. So you say 'Yes, yes, yes', and everybody exclaims, 'What a gentle creature you are, so strong in the Spirit you know.' Of course they don't mean it, but neither did you, so why complain?

You can also be gentle because you have a taste for emotional blackmail, and gentle weakness is strong stuff, if used cleverly.

You can also be really gentle, and hopelessly wrong, if you lack discrimination. If, for example, you are gentle to the wrong person, and hard on the right one. In this case the wrong person is usually yourself, and the right person someone else.

But sometimes you meet the real thing, that gentleness which is the fruit of the Spirit, and very disconcerting it is. It is quite ruthless, as love usually is. It is so uncalculating that you don't know where to put it or how to respond to it, so it makes you quite cross. It is so spontaneous and direct, there is no time to protect yourself with psychology or theology. It is so convincing that you know it can't be just natural, but something more – supernatural.

So instinctively you look up. And there's that crazy dove circling around overhead. 'Lord, make it descend on us!'

God lies in wait!

You do everything religiously right and God walks out on you. Then you do everything that seems religiously wrong and He walks back in again. That's how it was with me.

I was grateful when they gave me a scholarship to study for the ministry, and I willingly conformed to suburban ways to repay them. I admired them because they were responsible folk, not just respectable, who also gave their time as well as their money to charity.

But one day I had to face facts. As far as I was concerned, God had gone out of the system, and it was no use chasing Him round and round the liturgy.

So feeling fed up, I reverted to my old ways and joined some artists on their way to a rave-up in Copenhagen. Somewhere beyond Bremen our car dissolved into a cloud of rust, and the party began then and there. I wandered around town, and ended up in a decrepit caff by the docks.

And there I saw her! Elegant, chic, pure Paris and utterly out of place. When she agreed to dance, I couldn't believe my luck.

They were giggling their guts out at the other tables, and the penny dropped. She wasn't a she, but a he – not a homosexual but a transsexual, a woman in feeling, who'd been born into a man's body. 'Don't worry', whispered my friends. 'We'll get you out of this, we can hitch to Copenhagen without a car.' As I got up to go, the old familiar inner voice returned. 'Sit down!' it said. I sat down, surprised and relieved. 'Good boy!' said God.

I escorted her to the opera and to tea at smart hotels. Like many of her kind, she didn't want sex, only recognition of what she felt she was. Two years later, I heard she'd taken an overdose. I was grateful God had used me to give her a good time, because for people like her, life was even tougher than now and it had played her a dirty trick.

What did I get out of it? Not sex, as I've said, but sparkling conversation, and the envious looks of other men, which was a new experience. I also got back God!

If you've lost Him too, perhaps your religion has become too cosy. Perhaps He's waiting for you outside it – in your fears and theological doubts – in hot issues like women's lib and embarrassing ones like transsexuals, in Palestinian refugees if you're Jewish, and anti-Jewish prejudice if you're not.

Some elderly nuns were put out to grass, for quietness and contemplation. Instead they make meals and wash men's undies for AIDS sufferers. Their refectory has become a gymnasium for exercise and massage. That's how these nuns got back their youth.

If you come to a frontier, and play safe and refuse to cross it, then you can only return to banality and boredom. But if you go forward, and take the risk, and cry 'help' when you slip, then that's a real prayer, and that's how you get God back.

Wrong reasons for the right thing

Rabbi Zadok says: Do not use the Torah as a crown for your own importance or a spade to dig with.
                    (*Sayings of the Fathers*, ch. 4 v. 7)
And Joseph said unto them (his brethren), Fear not for am I in the place of God? But as for you, ye thought evil against me: but God meant it unto good . . .
                    (Genesis, ch. 50 v. 19–20)

When I decided to become a rabbi, I felt guilty because I had done the right thing for the wrong reasons. I no longer think right or wrong reasons important. Just as you cannot simulate a marriage, you cannot simulate a religious commitment either. You can call it a leap of faith or a pig in a poke, but you do not know what you are in for, until you are in it. It is not why you go in that is important, but what happens to you when you are in.

Some people I know commit themselves in one leap of faith to a religious organization and their problem is living with the consequence of that leap in the years to come. I am not a spiritual high-flyer. My family had stalls in a market, and England at its best has always been a nation of shopkeepers. I

55

retain a market trader's distrust, even when I deal in religious bargains. I am prepared to commit my ways to God if I have to, but I am not prepared to commit them to my fellow men, whatever robes they wear or whatever organizations they represent. This applies also to their Scriptures, their behaviour systems and their creeds. In spite of the fact that I have more and more regard for believers and their niceness, I prefer to learn from my own mistakes than from their successes – even if I have to pay the bill.

All the reasons I gave to the committee which accepted me for rabbinical training were true. I did want to translate the warmth and kindness of my traditional Jewish childhood into modern life. I did know that cleverness was not enough and that underneath it was a wisdom which could master me but of which I could not be the master. I knew that Judaism was my home. I also was quite clear that where prayer led I had to follow.

I was also aware that there were a lot of other reasons too, and, since they were shrewd men, they must have been aware of them also. Later on, the tables turned, and it was my turn to sit on seminary admission boards and on religious courts hearing applications for conversion. The following is an uncomfortable list of the 'wrong' reasons for coming to God or to the institutions which try to represent Him. Some of them were my own (some are still) and some are ones that even startled me. All of them combine with one another or with 'right' reasons, whatever they might be.

Getting a job. As I have said before, a religious vocation is a strong motive for displaced intellectuals. It is even stronger if you have an arts degree and yearnings after infinity.

Marriage is a common one, and a great deal of my present work is concerned with it. I give an example. She is Jewish, and you are not. Her parents are causing trouble and are hunting you with tribal tomahawks unless you get circumcized fast and convert. Where can you find an incompetent rabbi and a competent anaesthetist? ('Will it hurt?')

You are going to church or synagogue because you are a dutiful son or daughter. You have also realized that you can use your piety to sock your parents one in the eye – especially if you decide to become a monk or a nun, or to enter a religious college, or to convert. How on earth can they protest about your 'vocation' – the swines! They instinctively feel the aggression in your devotion, but in face of the divine they are out-manoeuvred. There are many cases with this element, and the strategy, even if unconscious, compels my admiration.

Frustration in love or sex is very common too, and takes many forms. You cannot get a boyfriend or girlfriend, so you settle for a divine one because there are no human ones around. Though God is above sex, His representations are not, so be careful about the brand of religion you choose. If you want a divine girlfriend, you are out of luck if you are a Jew or Protestant, and in luck if you are a Catholic or Hindu.

Another variant on this theme arises if you have fallen for your rabbi, pastor or priest, and have confused him with the Almighty. It is rather like transference in psychoanalysis. (As many modern ministers consciously try to be attractive and 'with it', they can be accomplices too.) The result is that you yearn to worship with him and prefer incense to musky after-shave (or, with the ecclesiastical emancipation of women, to perfume).

Another back door to religion is business or status. Joining the right church can put you in with the right people. In this context, 'right' is more political than theological. In communal religions this aspect becomes quite important. You can become a churchwarden or synagogue councillor, and get status that way, or you can give large sums to religious charities and buy it. This is a problem for all middle-class religious set-ups where there are hardly any working-class people, or if they exist they are the recipients of religion, not the donors – a sort of Marxism in reverse. Surveying the market, however, in a business-like way, I think becoming a Freemason would be more efficient. This is no aspersion on them, it is a side-effect of their success – their hospitals, charities and mutual help are quite outstanding.

Sadness and sorrow are good diving-boards into the divine. More of religion is based on them than on virtue and happiness. As there are more great tragedies than there are great comedies, it is the easier option. It is easier to be depressed or aggressive than patiently to work through a problem and solve it. Broadcast prayers have a dying fall, and their subject-matter in the morning does not help people facing a new day with as much cheerfulness as they can muster. (Lord, turn thy gaze on Bangladesh and its starving millions . . . Lord, we lay Northern Ireland and its problems before thee . . . Lord . . .) Sermons, too, have a querulous note. Even if the words betray some optimism, this is pricked by the mournful voice. This voice is worth noting, with its complaints and reproaches, because it has become a permanent feature of Western religion. Why this is so, I do not know. It is equally difficult to see how the common sense of Judaism and the freedom of the gospel resulted in all the sexual hang-ups and injustices of the early Middle Ages – yet a change took place in the first centuries of the Christian Era and it is not easy to account for it. Nietzsche saw clearly the weakness that underlay much religion. Like most young people, I read Nietzsche and then abandoned him because he was too querulous and too one-sided. Later I had to consider him again, because so much conventional religion was based on weakness, keeping the devotees in an unnaturally prolonged childish dependence and preventing their maturity. I have always liked the words of Ezekiel: 'Stand on your own feet, and speak!' I like Job's arguments more than his submission. If I could, I should prefer to approach divine things from strength and happiness. As it happens, I can't most of the time, and this is my own personal sin, a real one.

When people go to their dentist, their theology undergoes a profound change. People also pray when they are too embarrassed about their pains and problems: if they suspect they have got V.D., for instance, or are speedily about to become a one-parent family. '*In hac valle lacrimarum*' hits the nail on the head, and the 'vale of tears' is very recognizable.

To continue the gloomy tale, self-deception comes quite high on the list. Life seems dull, and religion of the charismatic variety certainly hots it up a bit. Some people go into the ministry because they like hearing the sound of their own voice and think a congregation might get the same glow. Religion is good for rhetoric, echo and reverberation. From pulpits, your voice can come back to you at all angles and at all volumes. You can turn it up, crescendo (God), or you can turn it down, diminuendo (humility, for example), and there is always some background wow and flutter provided by the choir. You can also deceive yourself at a deeper level. It is quite easy to visit a convent in the country, especially in summer, and decide to become a contemplative. There is a lot of knee-work, it is true, but there is no telephone, and you wear out less shoe-leather than running after the morning bus. You quite soon realize that what you need is a holiday, not a vocation. Thomas Merton says a contemplative monastery today is run on the lines of a munition factory in wartime. In the ones I visit, an extraordinary amount of manual labour goes on. You have to have a vocation to be a navvy or a builder's labourer as well.

Wives predominate over husbands among the clientele of prayer. I suppose instinctively they want to make the nest more secure and stop their husbands straying. (Men predominate in pubs.) In these uncertain times a Roman Catholic ceremony is still the best glue available, but even that is no longer cosmic Araldite.

A great deal of a minister's work involves counselling, and the range extends from the disorganized to the dotty. Most people are a bit neurotic, but they find it easier to present their neurosis in theological terms. Divinity makes you a little more interesting, and it certainly covers a lot of dottiness. It gets more dangerous when religion is a vehicle for megalomaniacs. 'Thou art That' and all that, or being part of the Mystical Body, or embodying the Jewish Problem.

A dangerous reason for becoming godly is to deepen one's nationalism or tribalism. It is a primitive and powerful combination. All detachment and holiness is gone when God is made to shout 'up the Irish' (or the English), or authenticate uncertain rights to promised lands.

I end this grim and dismal list, though the variations on it are infinite. I have never met anybody in my life who has entered religion pure and uncontaminated by any one of the above. I have met some people who thought they were not. I was curious about them. A few were liars, some had no insight about themselves and lacked self-awareness, others had hypnotized themselves out of truth.

Religion, real religion, begins when it can risk the truth. Conversion takes place when you can admit to yourself all the wrong reasons that are at work. For many years I tried to pretend to myself, and my God became pretence too and the awareness of Him make-believe. One day at a service, I said to myself 'To hell with it!', recognized the impurity in myself, and knew that I was not God's boy-scout. At that moment, when I became myself and admitted what I was, I could pray. At the time, I thought my reasons for going into religion were important. Now I believe that, when I was brave enough to admit they were the wrong reasons, I was right in applying. It sounds cock-eyed, but the truth digs deeper than our conventions.

Seven Deadly Sins on holiday

A new brochure has come out which is really plain-speaking and doesn't say 'refreshing' when it means 'rowdy', or 'lively' when it means 'noisy and you won't get to sleep until the early hours'. I study it carefully like the Bible, interpreting not only what it says but also what it doesn't say, which is even more important. Soon I shall be one of the packaged millions surging south, dreaming of sun and something else, on an undiscovered, exclusive costa on the Med – God help us! But brochures, however plain-speaking, aren't the cure for any disappointments, because we disappoint ourselves.

I recommend an old discipline. After you've collected your brochure, sit on a park bench or in a chapel and ask yourself if anything inside you spoils your happiness. If you're not sure how to begin, run through a checklist of the seven deadly sins to find out if they are the culprits – an old-fashioned but an effective test. This is a good practical spiritual exercise.

Start with VANITY, the most innocent and yet physically the most uncomfortable. Don't breathe in buying new jeans – the ones in daring pastel shades! On holidays you'll eat and drink more than at home and you'll end up like poor TV darts players whose pinnies can't hide their beer bellies. Also, who knows what will go pop at the hotel barbecue – a zip, the all-important top button? Choose something comfortable instead. People like comfortable partners. But if your pants do go pop, remain philosophical. Even in an age of women's lib, many need to be needed and will enjoy sewing you together behind a bush. So will some prospective gay partners. I speak as a man but the same applies to a woman and you can transpose the garments yourself.

GLUTTONY means not piling everything on your plate at the buffet and cementing the mess with mayonnaise. It's such a giveaway! You're either so old you remember the last war and consume anything in sight, or you're insecure and stuff yourself because the opportunity may never come again. It's also self-defeating. I saw a man with a tottering mountain of food on his plate and then he came to the last item, the special paella of the week. His tragic features showed he just didn't dare add it on. The other diners stayed their forks and speculated on the human tragedy. He left the buffet without his paella, a chastened gourmand!

Mental LUST doesn't seem so serious today. Few hide what they feel as boobs and bottoms parade by. But the difference between what you feel and what you do is civilization. Instead of complex theologies of sex, here are some simple practical summaries for your own happiness. Don't do in Benidorm what you'll regret in Basingstoke! Keep appointments! Avoid lies – even white ones!

PRIDE used to concern what you were, your class or your family. But now it's what you have that counts. Now, some fantasy of high life is part of any good holiday and most of us want a marble foyer or brandies at the bar to back it up. But don't let such frou-frou seduce you into a hotel with two stars too many. You won't be able to wander nonchalantly into the à la carte with your posh new friends but will have to return to the old set dinner instead because it's inclusive. The strain of putting on the style can be jolly hard work.

ENVY means totting up everybody else's package, to work out who got the best deal. But this becomes fiendishly difficult. In one you get free tea and biscuits and in another a lower supplement for SV (sea view). What's worth what? You grind your teeth in despair. And you won't be able to enjoy what you've got because you'll be so mad about what they've got and you haven't.

SLOTH means getting too heavy mentally and psychically as well as physically, lying in bed and letting everybody else do the work, like planning trips and buying tickets. Others will have to provide the sparkle, the entertainment, and they'll resent it. In the end they'll dump you. Why allow yourself to get so heavy inside?

AVARICE is a fancy way of being greedy, like an addiction. Some are addicted to food, some to sex, some to gambling, some to their neuroses, some to cigarettes, some to booze and some to repetitious praying. Whatever the compulsion, most people need help to get out of it. There's Alcoholics Anonymous and Over-Eaters Anonymous and Gamblers Anonymous. There's bound to be an Anonymous to fit you. Join it! Perhaps there's a Holidays Anonymous. You might prefer to work at home. Holidays can be the hardest work of all.

There's another sin, known as ACCIDIE, which is a kind of boredom, meaninglessness, listlessness. It often strikes at noon or in the afternoon. It's more common in affluent societies like ours than in the poorer ones of the past.

But, of course, for a happy holiday be prudent as well as virtuous. Like the family who booked into that gastronomic costa hostelry I've called 'Chez Rabbin Bleu'. 'How's the food?' asked a friend. 'Well, after the duck died,' mused the guest, 'we had superb Canard à l'Orange. And when the hen died, Poulet Henri Quatre. But yesterday Rabbin Bleu died and we went self-catering.'

Toothbrush and paste

She was old and derelict, her shoes squelched water and she had wrapped some newspapers under her blouse for warmth. She clung to my jacket and tried to bully me into buying a dud bracelet. It was New Year's Eve and I was in a pub celebrating. I fished out 80 pence from my pocket and put the coins on the table next to her.

Why? Well, if you're religious, you have to live with an itchy conscience. Also she reminded me of my grandma. Also I thought I might end up like that, and the money was a kind of insurance. Also I wanted to buy her off as I am fastidious.

Having done my duty, I moved away sharply with my glass to the other end of the bar where I could relax. While I sipped away, I suddenly thought of Colin, whom I hadn't thought about for years. You may have heard of him too, because before his death he became Bishop of Damaraland-in-exile, who celebrated communion in Trafalgar Square with hot gospel choirs.

When I got to know him at Oxford, the future bishop was flogging undies and cut-price nylons and what-have-you in the market during the vacation with my other mates, for all of us were up at Oxford on austerity grants.

Though I was revolutionary and Colin was religious, we decided to hitch-hike to Israel together, for ladies' lingerie was a link between us. Colin wanted to inspect relics and I wanted to witness revolutions, not the kind that was cooked up and then fizzled out in Oxford Junior Common Rooms.

We lurched across Europe, squeezed onto trucks, and got scarred for life on the top of gravel lorries. It was a relief when a hearse unexpectedly stopped for us in Burgundy. As the stately hearse seemed to be just right for religion, with my consent Colin had a go at converting me from Trotsky to the Church of England, but it was too big a jump and he hadn't yet had enough missionary practice. He lectured me on the apostolic succession. It seemed to be a chancy thing, like all life's goodies.

Some people had it, and some had just missed the boat. Colin was sure the Church of England had it, and he thought the Church of Sweden might have it too, transmitted by a Swedish Bishop of the Reformation, who Colin freely admitted was bonkers.

I put up with it because I had a Talmudic mind. But if Colin didn't teach me doctrine, he taught me some real religion. I was always losing things. Now, a lot of ethical people will lend you their toothpaste, but Colin lent me his toothbrush as well, and his least dirty socks and his sleeping-bag. I don't suppose all Anglican bishops are like that, which is understandable but a pity.

We finally went steerage on an old crock of a boat to the Holy Land. The officers told us to get off by the first-class gangway and, being prudent, that is what I did, but Colin refused. So a nice wee lassie welcomed me to the Holy Land with a cup of iced malted milk. Sipping it, I watched Colin come down with the ragtag and bobtail. He waved to me snootily and then disappeared like Moses in a cloud because someone stuck a nozzle down his shirt and deloused him. He looked a bit crestfallen, but I didn't say 'I told you so' because I realized then that he had a religious quality I lacked. I disliked poverty, but I didn't like poor people. Colin not only liked them, but he also tried to love their poverty as well.

Looking across the bar, I saw the old lady move somebody's abandoned glass in front of her, so that she could pretend to be a bona fide drinker and enjoy the smoky warmth till closing time. Thinking of Colin, I ordered two pints of bitter and took them over to her table. 'We'll drink to old friends', I said, and she blearily assented. It was better than a memorial prayer, and it seemed a sacramental way to start the New Year.

Badly used

When I was ordained I was so proud that I rushed to the synagogue and sat at my new desk in my new office waiting for my first clients. There was no great rush, but just as I was about to shut up shop, a man knocked at the door. He was about to commit suicide, he said belligerently, and what was I f——ing going to do about it!

I was startled and blurted out the first question in my mind. 'How are you going to do it?'

He stared at me in disbelief. 'What a question to ask!'

'Well, what am I supposed to ask?' I replied, sulkily.

'You gotta tell me how wrong it is, see', he said patiently.

'I can't very well,' I said, 'because when I tried it once, I bungled it.'

'I always do', he said compassionately. We looked at each other and rocked with laughter. I made tea and we spent a cosy evening discussing all possible methods. We illustrated our arguments with gestures.

At two in the morning he said he would have to go, as he was on early shift that day – that's life! But he had enjoyed himself, and I had done him a power of good.

Though such interviews seemed funny at first, I began to get disconcerted and then fed up with people who only wanted to use religion and me. When I got a job on the Continent, the same thing happened. But one day a Protestant minister asked to see me. Would I please unbaptize a hundred Jews and half Jews, he asked. He had handed out baptism certificates in Germany during the war, because this sometimes delayed their descent into the hell of the concentration camps.

'Were any of them really interested in Christianity?' I asked.

'Oh,' he said, 'how could I ask them, Rabbi Blue? It was wonderful for me at that time to be of use to anybody.'

From him I learned that allowing yourself to be used and even misused on occasion is what living and eternal living is about. (Don't overdo it – being a doormat doesn't help you, or anybody who tramples over you.) Everyone knows it who deals with such tricky creatures as human beings like us, psychiatrists as well as ministers.

So here is a story of a psychiatrist who saw a Jewish woman and her neurotic son. After examining the lad, the psychiatrist said to the mother, 'Well, I can't find anything wrong with your Abie, except for a somewhat overdeveloped Oedipus complex.'

'Ach, doctor,' she said, 'Oedipus, Shmoedipus, who cares, I don't! So long as he loves his mummy. Me!' she added firmly.

The gnat

The ministry is not a highly paid profession and many clerics find it hard to socialize in a middle-class congregation. They haven't got the means. So, like other low-paid professionals, they try to combine work with pleasure and have a free holiday by leading a pilgrimage party or attending and lecturing at a conference. This busman's holiday doesn't work well with me where the essence of a holiday is a complete cut-off from all the ordinary demands and preoccupations of my job, even from the people I know and minister to (except God), though I am very fond of them.

But whenever I travel and move out of my environment, my senses get sharpened and I notice things I would never have done at home. Does travel broaden the mind? With me certainly, though in very unpredictable ways. At one such ecumenical conference the predictable parts were pleasant and kind. Nice nuns explained their lives and vocations to Free Church people, and Evangelicals to Anglo-Catholics, while I explained to anybody who would listen what a Jew like me was doing among them. But a moment of unprogrammed enlightenment came to me from two creatures who didn't figure on the programme – a real gnat and a fictitious cow.

I noticed the gnat as I sat beside a lecturer and watched it trying to cross the table – though why, because there was nothing there for it on the other side? But then dogs also look as if they're trotting to urgent appointments, but they're so easily distracted by other dogs' bottoms you can't believe them.

This gnat seemed set on a pilgrimage of biblical proportions. It hesitated before a ravine between two piles of lecture notes. But then somebody asked a theological question, and the speaker shuffled his notes, nearly murdering my gnat, who now faced a cliff not a ravine. Every valley had been exalted for the poor insect, just as Isaiah prophesied.

I decided to make the crooked straight for the poor thing but it nearly fell off in alarm. I would never understand its thoughts – it would never understand mine. How could I explain to it, for example, the theology that had nearly murdered it? And yet are we human beings so different from gnats, crawling on the surface of a speck in space whose vastness and purpose are beyond our understanding?

I mentioned this sad fact to a Dutch delegate in the bar who tried to cheer me up with Dutch gin and jokes. 'How does the cow hunt a hare?' he asked. 'Well, how does it?' I replied obligingly. 'It hides behind a tree and pretends to smell like broccoli', he answered.

Perhaps you get it – I don't, and it wasn't the gin because I'd heard that joke before in Holland from a politician and a publisher. How little we know not just of gnats but of our nearest neighbours in the EU.

Although I didn't learn much from the fictitious cow, later on I did learn a lot from real ones. Reluctantly I had allowed myself to be persuaded to go on a cheap, self-catering, country holiday. It was not a success. I am a town person and need people to chat to. But a friend of mine who does like the country advised me to chat to my fellow creatures, though not my fellow human beings – cows, real ones!

I thought he was having me on, but he was right. They do get interested in their muzzy way when a human being talks to them and they gather round on the other side of the fence to listen. Of course they don't understand the details of what you're telling them, but they seem genuinely sympathetic and on your side, which is more than you can say about a lot of your fellow humans. I found talking to them very therapeutic, which made my unenthusiastic country holiday worthwhile. For the first time in my life I tried to understand the way they looked at life as they were trying in their dim fashion to under-stand mine. Do they resent us taking their milk, I wondered? Wasn't it intended for their calves? Such questions would never have come into my mind back home in a London super-market. Travel had undoubtedly broadened my mind, which is what it should do because your mind, as well as your body and soul, has to be satisfied on holiday.

Therefore I advise you to *exercise* your mind on holiday. Use it to cross a barrier of prejudice and increase understanding. Converse with Germans and gays and Americans, and Japanese with cameras. You wouldn't do it at home, but now is the opportunity. That is what travel is for, packaged travel, any kind of travel. Precisely because such learning is unprogrammed, we learn more. Looking back on a half-century of holidays, it is the memory of conversations in trains, in hotel foyers and on dusty roads that have remained with me. They were my education. Risk it!

Postscript

In 1785, a nest of mice was dug up during the ploughing of a field. Robert Burns learned sad lessons of life from their fate.

> But Mousie, thou art no alane
> In proving foresight may be vain.
> The best laid schemes o' mice and men
> Gang aft agley.

Cigarette and Handbag

In tense times, people not unnaturally turn to God, but that's easier said than done. 'Where can I find God, for religious rituals have gone dead on me?' becomes a practical, not an academic, question.

It's happened to me too. I couldn't find Him either in all the old familiar places. Now the prophet Jeremiah said play holy hide-and-seek with Him. ' "If you seek Me you will find Me. If you seek Me with your whole heart, I shall let you find me" says the Lord.'

Tracking Him down seemed to me more like a holy treasure hunt than hide-and-seek, and two incidents provided the clues.

The first took place in the waiting room at the end of a hospital ward. The doctors were doing their rounds, so I sat waiting with two women. One woman fumbled with her handbag, the other smoked cigarette after cigarette. They weren't aware of each other.

Then Sister poked her head in and beckoned to Cigarette. 'You can see your husband now, Mrs So-and-so – I'm afraid you'll find him rather sleepy.' Cigarette went out and returned ten minutes later. She hesitated and then went over to Handbag, which intrigued me, and impulsively tapped her on the arm. 'Your turn now. No, I won't come in with you. See him alone.' Handbag, looking astonished, scuttled out, while Cigarette sat on motionless. Something significant had happened, but what?

Later on I learned that the man was dying. Cigarette was his wife, Handbag his mistress.

I'd witnessed an act of spontaneous generosity. Cigarette had let God get into the act as well as her rival, and I don't think she would ever regret it. The glow certainly remained with me for months.

That incident made me think of a funeral on the Continent. The mourners were grave, the prayers moving, and the sermon solemn, theological rather than personal, in the continental manner. It was a cold day and the rawness of death made me shiver.

Later on I learned the deceased had AIDS, though this was never mentioned. Not mentioned either were his friend and his buddy, both of whom had been discreetly advised to stay away, though it was they who had nursed him, wiped away the sweat from his face and held him tight when he felt hopeless.

God must have been with them, when they nursed him, I thought, otherwise they couldn't have done it. But like them, I don't think He attended that funeral either, which accounted for my sense of desolation.

A rabbinic story helped me interpret these two clues. A rabbi was asked, 'Where does God live?', the same question, in another form, that I mentioned before. 'Wherever a human being lets Him in', he answered.

And I would add two things I learned from these incidents. His presence brings no quick worldly triumphs – just the glow I mentioned – and the password to His presence is generosity. So it's up to you whether you want to pay the price and let Him into your life – advice which is hard but hopeful.

The case of the bearded bride

I once went to a monastery at Christmas. Word came down from above that we should 'rejoice', and, being an obedient lot, we tried very hard to be light and spontaneous. We spoke at table, we clinked glasses and toasted each other in thick, sweet, tonic wine. We laboriously told jokes, though we were so anxious to draw the line that we lost the point. It was great – we all said so.

It was a relief next day to get back to the penitential life, to listen in cosy, gloomy silence to the sayings of superior saints, and to extinguish the awful aftertaste of that wine with strong stewed tea. At last we were able to feel glum again, which is a reasonable response to life, and an old monk told me in private that he was tearful with joy now that the party was over and he could meet God again.

In this he was mistaken for, since God is everywhere, when you go to a party, He goes too, the divine gatecrasher.

The rabbis of old knew quite well that the Almighty was interested in parties. When I was a student for the ministry, prodded on by my teacher, I brooded for weeks over the following rabbinic problem. At Jewish weddings it is customary, indeed it is obligatory, to go up to the groom and tell him what a lovely bride he's got. Now, say your best friend invited you to his wedding, and just as you were about to tell him what a lucky chap he was and what a beautiful bride he had, you peeked and suddenly realized she had a beard. What can you say in all honesty about a bearded bride?

The rabbis agonized over this and one of them thought he had found the way out. She might, he said, look somewhat queer in the eyes of man, but perhaps she was a pious woman and beautiful in the sight of God. So, therefore, there was no problem. Go up to your friend and slap him on the back and say, 'Old boy,' or whatever the equivalent is in ancient Aramaic, 'what a beautiful bride you've got.'

But the rabbis of old were not cowards. Unlike more modern clerics, they preferred to face a problem head on. So they insisted on asking the awkward question: what if she has no spiritual beauty either, what if she is not only bearded but loose? So what do you say to your friend if you go to the party and find he has just married a hirsute harlot?

Now this is a serious matter. Do you spoil the party or tell a white lie? In all my studies this is the only instance I have found when the rabbis were prepared to relax the rules of strict honesty. To save the party and spare the newly married couple and everyone else a social disaster, they gritted their teeth and said, 'You go up to your friend with his hairy love beside him, and without batting an eyelid you tell him what a lovely bride he has got – and God help you if you snigger.'

So chin chin, your health and halleluyah!

A whiff of adultery

If you're wise you will realize that jokes are not always joking matters and that God can reveal His hand at a cocktail party as well as on a mountain top.

I'm going to tell you about a joke I heard at a party and the commentary on it the party provided, which I've thought about a lot, though it was really quite a trivial incident.

Three of us were standing together near the tit-bits. I had gravitated towards another clergyman, for clerics huddle together for mutual protection at parties. Lots of people don't know how to treat ministers. Some go on and on about the state of their souls, and they feed you with little scraps of Jung or such. And you have to look a bit surprised and soulful and say, 'Yes, yes, it's too, too divine', or something equally ambivalent.

The other lot feel compelled to prove that you've got feet of clay, as if you didn't know it. So they tell you smutty stories, and you're trapped. If you laugh, you're smutty too, and if you don't, you're impolite. In my case, you've heard them before – told much better by your colleagues.

With us was a lady who had joined us, I suppose, because she wasn't paired off. She was in good form, though I knew she had had a rough time. Anyway, she was sympathetic and brought out the best in us. I told a harmless joke from the Old Testament, and the Christian minister capped it with one from the New. It's not a disrespectful one, so I can repeat it, and in any case I had already heard a Jewish version of it about a saintly rabbi.

It was about the incident in the Gospels concerning the woman who came to Jesus possessed by seven devils. Just as he was about to heal her and expel her devils, she whispered urgently, 'Master, may I have a word with you, may I make a special request?'

'Of course,' he said, 'tell me.'

'Can I tell it to you very privately?' she added.

'Of course', he said again, and bent down, putting his ear close to her mouth.

She whispered into it softly, 'Only six, please.'

We laughed and exclaimed how terrible it would be if we lost our devils all at once. Who would ever invite us to parties again?

The lady left us to chat to an old acquaintance, a man, who had just arrived. He was also in good form and the lady began to sparkle as her appearance was admired and her wit appreciated, and I was pleased for her.

Later on, I glanced up. Another woman had joined them, and I was puzzled because the lady had fallen silent. She was listening quietly, just putting in an occasional remark. It was the newcomer who had begun to do the talking. I supposed she had put my friend's nose out of joint, so I went over to comfort her.

But she saw through my artless manoeuvre immediately and

said in an amused way that she wasn't yet ready for the con-
solations of the clergy. 'If you're a single woman,' she said, 'and
you get on well with an attractive man, you always sense the
first faint whiff of adultery in the air. As soon as his wife came
over, I knew I had to help her, let her shine and take a back seat
myself.

'I've been thinking, Rabbi, about that joke we heard, you
know that one about the bit of devilry the woman kept back. A
bit of devilry is OK provided you realize it's not a tabby cat
you're playing with but a tiger. That's how I lost my husband.

'Good day, gentlemen. Nice meeting you. I did enjoy your
jokes.'

Louis and Lottie

I first met her about 20 years ago. She was clothed in a black bombazine pup tent and on her head she wore a stiff starched white creation, like the frills on lamb chops, though she was not lamb but tough mutton.

With a slight guttural accent, she informed me her name was Sister Louis Gabriel, which seemed improbable, as she remained a German-Jewish refugee to the end of her days.

She also didn't look at me directly, but averted her eyes, which made her appear shifty. Perhaps she was overcome, I thought, at meeting a real rabbi and felt guilty about her conversion to Christianity.

I underestimated her completely. She had seen her synagogue set on fire in Berlin. She had married unsuccessfully, and fallen in love successfully. She had also fallen into the arms of the Church, and since she did nothing by halves, become a Catholic nun in Jewish Jerusalem teaching Arab children. She had been rescued by an Italian princess who had shipped her to Palestine, and there she had worked for British Intelligence. Having faced Nazis, Fascists and clerical disapproval, one immature rabbi was nothing to her. Being shifty wasn't in her nature; she was just being thorough and old-time, and keeping custody of her eyes.

She told me she disapproved of converts. People should stay in the religion where God had put them.

I swallowed hard, and said gravely, 'Except you of course.'

'Of course', she answered without batting an eyelid.

I saw Sister Louis Gabriel some years later after she came back from America. 'I am no longer called Louis,' she announced, 'but Lottie, my birth name.'

Sister Lottie was into liberation theology from Central America and wore long pants, which she had battled for at a Harrods sale.

She was as thoroughly modern as Sister Louis had been old-time. She puffed at a cigarette in a long holder while she sipped a weak whisky 'on the rocks'.

'Lionel, why don't you have a highball?' she said.

'Louis,' I said, 'no, Lottie, what on earth happened to your habit?'

'Hm . . . Let them use it for demonstrations', she said. She also gave me a book she had written about anti-Jewish prejudice in the Church. It didn't surprise me that she wasn't the establishment's favourite nun. It was a courageous book which said things that needed saying and only Louis/Lottie cold have said them. Being a German-Jewish refugee was tough. Being a German-Jewish refugee who became a Catholic nun was even tougher.

She taught me that religion was not about security or popularity, it was about courage, and witnessing to the truth as you knew it, not as someone else had told you you ought to know it. She was the only person I've ever met who could interrupt a sermon and say, 'Father, this is not so!' – something I've always wanted to do but never dared.

I used to collect refugee jokes for Charlotte and saved this one for her, a version of which I had heard from her friend Rabbi Gryn.

Two Jewish refugees in Wisconsin debated as to how you pronounced it. Was it Wisconsin or Visconsin? In the synagogue they asked a warden which of them was right.

'Oh, it's Visconsin,' he said, 'no doubt about it!'

'Thank you', they replied gratefully.

'You're velcome', he said as he waved them goodbye.

Before I could tell it to her, she died. Jesuits and Dominicans said a requiem Mass for her. Rabbis said Kaddish for her, and Sisters and unbelievers, addicts and the alcoholics she had helped, mourned for her.

Sister had guts!

The birds of Torremolinos

It was absurd! On the Costa del Sol in the height of summer, I was feverish with flu. At first I was confined to my hotel room, but later I was let out on the balcony, where I read the Bible, the only book the hotel could provide, and contemplated the long line of luxury hotels and crumbling concrete which slopes away from Torremolinos to Marbella, where the money is. It isn't my favourite costa, but then it doesn't cost a lot.

I felt fragile but content on my balcony. There was a table with two chairs, some shade to cool my bottles and, like a box at the opera, it overlooked Carihuela beach, where it all happens – 'it' being sex. One evening I watched the performers below. Their colour ranged from agony red to painful pink. Golly, I thought, how do they do it? If anyone touched me, I'd hit the roof. But no one did, and I went to bed.

Next morning I stopped reading the Second Book of Samuel while I was munching croissants and peered down at them. The beach was littered with bottles, and the embers of fires still glowed. But there was no glow of love left in the revellers. The girls sat sulkily on one side and their boyfriends looked mean and uncertain on the other.

In my feverish state, I imagined my balcony as a pulpit,

St Francis had preached to the birds. Well, I would preach to the birds below and their boyfriends. I leant over and addressed them as follows:

Dear birds and boyfriends. I am not going to burden you with my own morality. My life has not been so holy that I can pontificate over yours. So I shall turn to the Bible and take as my text the Second Book of Samuel, starting at Chapter 13, verse one. I shall read the lesson summary aloud, as you may not have brought your Bibles to the beach.

'Absalom, the son of David, had a fair sister, named Tamar, and Amnon, the son of David, loved her. And he pretended to be sick, and said let my sister come to my bed and feed me cakes. And when she brought them, he was too strong for her, and forced her and lay with her. And then he hated her with more hatred than the love with which he had loved her.'

The psychology and the message of this story still rings true. Never do anything the night before which makes you hate or despise your partner or yourself the next morning. It is very basic but very true, and much morality is based on it.

So endeth my sermon to the birds and their boyfriends.

On the beach, the birds scarcely noticed me – but a boyfriend did, and he heaved a bottle half-heartedly in my direction. I moved inside smartly, before he could hurl anything else. St Francis got better treatment from his birds, but that's the difference between life and legend, isn't it?

Marbella (where the money is!)

I want to warn you, not about the sufferings life inflicts on us, but about the unhappiness we inflict on ourselves.

On the Costa del Sol, my fever had gone, and I joined the holiday-makers by the beach. Large blonde ladies overflowed their bikinis, girls from Bradford plotted to capture a José or Jaime. Holiday home touts promised the freehold of Paradise, and an old man of 90 sashayed along, held up by his truss.

I suddenly thought I recognized someone there, an acquaintance, not a friend. I recognized his neighing, braying laugh.

Puzzled, I turned to examine the coach trips on offer. One promised the fountains of Granada. Another the cathedral at Cordoba. And another said, 'Come to Marbella – Where the Money Is'. What was it like to be wealthy? I was curious. So was an OAP called Doris, and we went together.

As we neared Marbella, our guide inflamed us with its marvels. 'Be careful in cafés – the prices!' He pursed his lips and pressed his finger tips together. We narrowed our eyes and nodded. 'Greenbacks, gelt, the old payola.'

But this made Doris bolshie. 'Don't worry, Rabbi – I'll save up for a down payment on two cuppas.' The guide glared and pointed to a blank wall. 'A famous celebrity lives here', he hissed. 'What's she famous for?' asked Doris. 'She's famous for being a celebrity.' 'I bet they're all bank robbers', said Doris disparagingly.

There was indeed more marble in Marbella – and more credit companies. But in the café Doris was despondent. 'Why, they're no different from us.'

Again I heard the neighing, braying laugh and recognized the Tempter. The Costa was his sort of place. Don't the rabbis say 'The Tempter goes about the world, thrusting his closed fist before people's faces. Guess what's in it, he taunts them. And people think it's what they want most, and die to get it. Then the Tempter opens his fist and laughs, for there's nothing there.'

I listened to the conversations at tables around me. 'We didn't get on in London, but it'll be different in our holiday home – I know it.'

'Yes, he's called Hosey. He works as a waiter, but he's a film producer really, and he'll wait for me 'til I come back next Christmas.'

'If only I had a room on the fourth floor, I would be really happy.'

The Tempter was having a field day. I wanted to warn them with another rabbinic text, but didn't.

'People long for things that cannot help them, and are frightened of things that cannot hurt them – for it is something inside themselves they're afraid of, and something inside themselves they long for.'

Spiritual walkabout

My friend Evie and I got hooked on spirituality and every so often, disillusioned with London life and the ecclesiastical rat race, went on spiritual walkabout round the country, calling in on surprised monasteries, convents and retreat houses to graze in fresh green spiritual pastures. Were we Christian? No. Were we married? No. Were we . . . ? No, we weren't that either. Most of them took us in and, as they had enormous buildings with few novices, allotted us floor space for our spiritual quest.

Occasionally we caused panic. 'My God, 'tis a woman', you could hear some think and, after much whispering, I would be assigned a cellar at one end of the monastery and Evie a turret at the other – which was kind, as they were old and we were odd and disturbing.

At teatime, all mumbles ceased ominously as Evie entered and sat down at the all-male refectory table. 'May I have some bread and butter?' she asked. 'No', croaked an ancient, and the other ancients cackled and waited to see whether they had driven her away. But Evie continued her tea obstinately in the hostile silence.

After meditating in the chapel, I found Evie had pinched my aftershave. She was having a ball. 'O you poor dears', she cried as the wrinklies chatted round her and she listened attentively and brushed and clipped their beards, removing egg stains from their dirty habits, polishing their nails pink with her manicure set, and sprinkling them with my aftershave. They purred with pleasure. At her insistence I told them about a teacher who asked his class who was the first woman in the world. 'I'll give you a clue,' said the teacher, 'it's an apple.' 'Granny Smith', shouted one boy proudly. The ancients fell about with laughter. Though properly watered and fed, no woman had cared for them lovingly, and unloved old men get surly and unkempt, just as unloved old women get finickety and spikey.

Evie couldn't make our next spiritual walkabout. She was too preoccupied with a sheep she had bumped into in a high street after midnight. Was it a pet or would she have to save it from sacrifice or the pot, perhaps I could help her? Life with her was like *The Perils of Pauline*.

But before she died I had learned from our last spiritual walk-about that the spirituality we seek is already inside us, otherwise we wouldn't want to make such a trip in the first place – the people we meet only trigger it off. Also she had retaught me a truth nearly forgotten in the new fashionable fanaticism with its hunger for religious results, that religion, whatever its theology, sociology, buildings, texts or titles, has to be validated by acts of loving kindness; otherwise it is hollow. Such acts are its heart.

Lunatic but loving

The train rushed through Rugby and swept on to Salford. I saw some cooling towers on the horizon and asked the man in the next seat if I could lean over and look through the window. He seemed surprised because it wasn't tourist country, just midlands' mess, but I wanted to see my old retreat house before they closed it in a year's time and it was turned into a supermarket, or a holiday home, or a hamburger heaven, or a superior hotel or a lunatic asylum.

The building was rather lunatic, built in Victorian times and ornamented tastefully with turrets, towers and minarets, no expense spared. It was lovely, like St Pancras Station. It had long echoing corridors, just right for a game of murder, and more stonework than a suburban cemetery.

The building rested on a coal mine, though rested is not the right word because it never stood still. The canal which I looked down into on my first visit, I looked up at on my last. Holes could open at your feet, which provided sermon subjects of the sadder sort. One day the lake leaked out through a crack and a merciful muddy monk dashed about rescuing grubby, gasping fish.

The friars there tried to trust people, which is not lunatic but unexpected. Sometimes they got stung, but not often, and I learned there that people rise to the occasion and become what you believe they are. They gave the rabbis the key to the bar and told them to tot up the totals themselves. They let you meander on about mysticism in the kitchen at midnight, and didn't measure out the marge or count the cups of tea. Their trust worked wonders. At the bar a lively group socialized amiably with members of a cricket club, and rabbis found refuge in a jam session, playing the kazoo.

You weren't chivvied in the chapel if you were on a retreat, or made to run a lap round the liturgy. Instead they just let the Lord find you – and, for me, He did just that.

They also treated religious people as adults, which is rare. I heard a priest sermonize to some novices on prayer, and I waited for the pious patter. I heard this instead: 'Prayer is an adventure. You hope it might help your vocation. I hope so too. But it might lead you out of your vocation into the unknown. You must take the risk.' This was the hard stuff and I didn't miss another word.

He who hesitates

I have begun to realize that I must go away on a retreat again. My religious instinct tells me it is time. What surprises me always is the strength of my other instincts which tell me to do no such thing.

Over the years, I have learned to stand back from this battle of the instincts and to watch the struggle appreciatively with some detachment.

The anti-retreat voices begin with their objections, which start off by being very high-minded. 'You have no time for such things', they say. 'Judaism is a religion of this world and you must sit at your desk and overfulfil your norm. Religion means serving society.'

I consider this, but ask myself what it means in practice. Sitting on more committees? Arranging more religious divorces?

The anti-voice then continues: 'God is everywhere – you know that there is no need to go to some God-forsaken hole in rural England in December. You can find Him (or Her) just as well with the central heating at home, can't you?' Of course, I know I can find God everywhere, but in practice I don't. I also find in prayer that I have to take a step towards God, before He takes two steps towards me. Stepping into the unknown (even if it is a very safe and secure unknown) is the best way of invoking His presence. 'So,' the anti-voice continues, 'you insist on being so gentile. All this prayer and inner life, what is it but romantic subjectivity?' The inner life, I agree, hasn't been a feature of the Jewish life I've known, which has been a mixture of liturgy, communalism and committees. But I remember that the rabbis of old meditated for hours before their prayers, and I think of the inner conversations in the Hebrew Scriptures and I know that I am not the odd-man-out in Jewish tradition.

'Don't you think,' says the anti-voice, 'that counselling would be more scientific? You could do that better in London.' 'Well, yes,' I reply, 'knowledge of myself and knowledge of God have to go hand in hand or I shall become a fanatic or make God in my own image, but the former does not replace the latter. God is within me, but my ego does not limit Him (or Her).'

Listening to this inner argument, I wonder what it is I am afraid of, what I am avoiding. Is it that nothing will happen in prayer, or that something will happen? Either way causes complications. Religious experience isn't necessarily nice. It can mean facing yourself as you are. But emptiness can be worse. Perhaps I had better not put my religion to any sort of test. It might not be able to stand it.

But if I don't, what am I left with? The rat race, success and failure in worldly terms, and none of that great reserve of power and courage which has always helped me, wobbler though I am.

The anti-voice is not done yet, and now it gets to basics.

'You won't like it there', it says. 'The heating will be sparse, and the tea too strong. The prayers will be too long and the food will be stodgy with too many calories, and you are already overweight. You won't get any smoked salmon where you are going.'

But my other voice also speaks. 'All this is trivial stuff. OK, you won't get smoked salmon, but you'll get things that matter. Some companionship in that part of religion where it really counts. The friendship of God is like any other. If you neglect a friendship and don't speak or meet for a long time, you get out of the habit, and the friend becomes a stranger. If God becomes a stranger, it doesn't affect your public life, of course. You'll be able to gas on about religion and it might be quite popular. (People prefer synthetics.) But it will be gas, or like a cheque that has no money to back it, or like a public personality, or an empty conventional promise.'

The prospect of becoming a fraud to myself is more than I can bear. I pack up my little suitcase and slip in a detective story and a half-bottle of homemade wine. As I get towards the station, I feel that lightness which comes from not giving in.

My inner journey

Why does a one-time Marxist and a reformed rabbi like me mess around with nuns and monks and priories? Because they bring out the meditative and contemplative feeling side of me. Mystical is too big a word and I don't measure up to it. Now, I didn't want to be a nun or a monk or believe like them, but I still felt part of their company. Meditation and contemplation were not prominent preoccupations of Reform Jews in the 1970s – indeed any Jews. We were into social action, Israel, communal welfare and congregational expansion. It was only at the turn of the century, two or three decades later, that spirituality and religious experience began to catch on, though often misunderstood as emotional entertainment. People began to hum a lot to atavistic soul music.

I did need, if not a community, companionship on my own inner journey. You can feel an awful fool chatting to someone who isn't there and basing your life on a meeting with a See Through. I needed others who understood what I was trying for and why it was important because they were doing the same things themselves. More than me they were entrusting their lives to such inner conversation, such meetings.

A Discalced (no shoes) Carmelite Priory became a sort of

religious home and refuge for me and still is intermittently after 30 years. In London I had several worlds to integrate, partners (I had three in succession but not together), mother, aunt, a few congregations and a dog to look after. In the Priory chapel the confusion of calls didn't get resolved but their tensions oozed out of me and I was able to let an inner life well up in me and seem to speak in me. I needed a break, so it was a combination of vacations and vocation.

Why did I light upon a priory in the country when I wasn't a Christian, Catholic or countryman, I don't know. But I wasn't completely in charge. It takes two to tango, whether it's ballroom dancing, praying or passion. You might decide you'll meet the Holy Ghost (Old Smokey to intimates) at a certain time in a certain chapel or other recognized meditative venue, but Old Smokey may have very different ideas. To me he has been very accommodating. Since he accompanied me to sauna baths and bars in Amsterdam, it seemed only fair that I should accompany him to a Carmelite priory in the country which is not the place I myself would have chosen. But fair's fair whether the friendship is human or heavenly.

I was waiting to get a 'call' from somewhere but I didn't know where or how it would happen. I needed some spiritual stiffening to help me cope with bureaucratic religious formalism, my domestic muddle and my needs as a carer. Well, it happened in a way which took me off guard – as 'calls' do.

Now, I have my reservations about these Catholic-style 'calls' and indeed about official Catholicism itself. I don't approve of the silence of the Vatican during the Holocaust while it was actually happening. The least you expect of any decent religious establishment, including my own, is to point out the evil in front of your nose. Not even to mention it took some doing. I was not impressed. Nor was I impressed as a homo. Too many of my kind had been burned and tortured by it for me to feel neutral. Though these brutalities had stopped, we were still demonized, though this was covered by suspiciously sweet words of concern. I also thought the ecclesiastical policy on condoms irresponsible.

Gradually, thanks to Old Smokey, I simmered down. I realized that you don't have to swallow a religion or an ideology whole in one gulp. As in everything else, you have to discriminate. Other parts of Catholicism became enormously important to me, and the open chapels and churches, the lovely listening nuns, the friendly jokes and pieties and above all the religious orders, especially the contemplative ones. Of course the organizations say you can't pick and mix, but then they would say that, wouldn't they?

I was at the Dominican Centre at Spode when a call to move on came to me about 35 years ago, about 1970 I think. I got chatting to a stern Carmelite father who seemed startled when I casually and publicly mentioned my depressions and break down. After my residence in Greenwich Village, Holland, I wasn't prepared to play other people's games any more. I had crawled out of the closet and, though I knew I had to be cautious ('innocent as a dove but subtle as a serpent'), I would never be lured into it again with its fibs and half-truths.

In any case, such confessions might be hush-hush in priories, but they are standard fare in Jewish north-west London, where everyone is analysing or counselling everyone else. (Try co-counselling if you haven't got the funds.) I thought the Carmelite disapproved of me (I thought everyone did – my paranoia) but later on he came up to me and of course he was also a member of the introspective 'club', though not for the same reasons as me. After that we got on famously and he invited me to his priory near Oxford. As my projected visit wouldn't happen until eight months later, I didn't take it seriously. But the date sidled up on me. So one day, forlorn and fretful, trapped in the trap of my own too easy enthusiasms, I drove through snow and rain to Cold Comfort Farm country, gazing balefully at sodden fields, dripping trees, sad cows and frozen fences.

The smell of the place put me off. Every religion has its smell, its own odour of piety, and this was not the Madame Rochas or Charlie favoured by my mother, not even the wine, fried fish and strudel odour of Jewish piety. It was the Catholic combination of greens, lard and furniture polish, with whiffs of incense. My twitching nose told me I was too far from home.

The reading at dinner nearly sent me back home straightaway. I could hardly believe my ears but it was an account of the rallies organized by Schacht for Hitler. I later learned that one of the fathers had decided they ought to keep in touch with contemporary life and one of them had casually taken down Schacht's autobiography at random from the library shelves, not knowing what it was all about. It was a mean trick to play on a paranoid Jew. It took me several days before I got over my paranoia (justified this time) and summoned up the courage to enquire about such a bizarre selection. But then they were Irish, not Jewish, and saw the world in a different sort of way. It was the first time I had encountered Celtic culture in depth. For me piety meant 'Go east young man, go east!' to my roots, to whatever remained of the Yiddish holy cities of Eastern Europe. Now I had to think westwards to Ireland and Gaelic and a different set of persecutions, prayers, suppressions, voluntary privations, loves and hates – all very strange country for me. I had encountered a little of it in Bede's Ecclesiastical History but nothing as immediate, passionate and as concentrated as this.

The third put-off was the cold. They were just rebuilding the old house as a priory and the stables as a chapel. After working in the centrally heated Continent, this was a physical as well as a culture shock. I undressed by taking off my shoes but nothing else, not even my overcoat, and the next morning for the dawn meditation I just washed the tips of my fingers and squirted a quarter bottle of aftershave over me to suppress my body odours. The community of course endured the same deep freeze as me but with no aftershave. We all must have had a gamey unkempt air. Our odours combined curiously. I was reminded of my Amsterdam sauna.

I didn't turn round and go home, even after listening to Dr Schacht, but stayed on for a variety of reasons, difficult to disentangle, some this-worldly, some other-worldly. This-worldly ones first!

The fathers and brothers liked me, which made me blossom. Being human, not superhuman, I liked being liked. After the crises and rejections in my love life, this supported me just when I needed it. A tame Jew was also a rare acquisition – not every Catholic contemplative set-up had one. My vanities amused them. I am sure some of them eyed me speculatively as likely conversion material and whenever I appeared, screwed up their eyes hopefully in prayer. I figured this out myself because they never mentioned anything to me about conversion, of course, being true gentlemen. So I couldn't tell them that my mother was probably praying against them and she was a very determined lady.

I also liked the order of it all. I liked marching into the dining room in order. Rabbis came after fathers but before brothers. I also liked being read to at meals – it's one of the great luxuries in life and I was sorry it went some years after Vatican II. Misplaced modernism! Small talk is hard work, but being read to is bliss, especially when it was Peter Brown's book on Augustine. Actually I even liked the cold up to a point. Crucifying my flesh in moderation made me feel authentically monkish. They also understood the needs of prayers and meditators, both of which activities make me very hungry. All love makes me hungry! So they thoughtfully provided slabs of bread, marge and jam immediately afterwards to appease this professional need for calories. Also I had a great deal of innocent fun – better than the non-innocent kind, I decided. I enjoyed their homemade beer, playing ludo, eating curried bits (parsnips, porridge, etc.), telling edited Jewish jokes (censoring the blasphemous and raunchy ones).

Later on I returned in summer. It was a golden summer, and in memory I often re-experience it. It was one of the blessed times of my life. And I have returned to the Priory again and again for 30 years or more, never staying long, just two or three days at a time. I shall continue to do so as long as Old Smokey wants me to and I need him and they let me. I still need him and perhaps always shall.

The Priory has changed in exteriors. The chapel is complete now. It is pleasant and straightforward and the retreatants now dwell in heated cheerful chintzy rooms. They are also less exotic than some of the old lot of droppers-in. I miss the chap who kept a little suitcase of relics stowed under his bed. I bought one, a real bargain, but my cleaning lady, back home, fell in love with it and the spirit of the relic seemed to tell me to give it to her because she believed in it. Which I did and regretted immediately because being now relicless I missed it more than I thought. There were also some ladies trying to set up a new religious order. They breathed deeply in prayer, wore copious wimples and could kneel longer than the rest of us. I was touched by the courteous accepting way the fathers and brothers treated the poor dears, respecting their high spiritual aims. They treated me like that too!

For all of us, whatever our competence or condition, the chapel was central. (It reminded me of the Jewish *stiebels*, the prayer rooms of my childhood, which I went to occasionally with my father before breakfast.) It provided the meaning and purpose of our visits. It provided me with two qualities not easily found in Jewish life: privacy and silence. And also a place where chatting to non-material, see-through beings such as Smokey was not considered a *prima facie* case of schizoid tendencies but a normal activity. I sometimes delayed entering it because I wanted to intensify the pleasure. It was as much my home as Yiddish London.

At the beginning I tried hard, too hard. As with Marxism, anarchism and Orthodox Judaism, I tried to believe more than my capacity for the extraordinary – and how extraordinary so much of it is. Just as I thought I was beginning to swallow it, I metaphorically retched it all up. At first I tried to think this was my sin but then I relaxed and decided it was my sanity.

I also tried to force myself on Smokey, getting more intimate and pi than was my wont. He didn't respond and I don't blame him.

To ascend higher I used to gaze at a novice who gazed enraptured at the altar and tried to ride piggy back on his faith, which was obviously so much deeper than mine. It helped. Later on, after he left the novitiate and returned to normal life, I told him and thanked him. He burst into laughter because he had suffered from self-doubt like me and had delayed his departure because of the spiritual raptures he saw on my face. It was interesting how we had ascended piggy back on each other's piety, neither of us believing that much. God works in curious ways.

But my attitudinizing died down and my mental fights with Faith, which I don't have much of and never will, though I have trust, and I stopped trying to believe what I didn't believe and didn't make religious experience happen. Then I did begin to touch a peace within me and I began to see my contradictory, contrary life in perspective and learned to listen to my soul, not just my mind. I think I am making the prayer experience more cosy than I felt it at the time. Sometimes I was shocked by the intensity of God's anger and He appeared to me not as benign, but reaching out to me covered with blood. I do not know on what level to take this but I cannot wish it away.

Perhaps I was working too hard at this spiritual business. Since it takes two to tango, as I've said, it was time to let my Smokey partner take the initiative and do some of the work himself. I should talk less and let myself listen. I think this is what the chapel taught me. Just to ask God to be present to me and then leave Him to it. Yes, I know from experience the layers I have to get through. Wondering whether I've turned the gas off and let the cat in, or suddenly remembering all the embarrassing moments of my life, or where I've put my ticket home. And then there's the self-pity layer and the anger layer and only then my mind and my emotions stop rabbiting on and on and on and I give up. And then when I've given up trying to be a good boy or an ersatz Carmelite, then something touches me or Smokey whispers something funny but rude to me and I pass into the non-sensible dimension that encloses this world. It sometimes feels like coming home or pausing before the door of a closed garden and watching it swing open. One of the fathers I told this to told me to go through the door, but so far I never have.

The chapel, as well as being an opportunity, can also be a very subtle diversion because chapels and services create expectations and then once again you're back in the success game, whether it's labelled spiritual or not. Success for me is knowing I'm back on spiritual home ground or just saying to God, 'I'm very tired – over to You!'

I shall always have a problem going to Carmel. I tell myself that God is everywhere, so why do I have to get to Paddington, the most inconvenient London station for me. Also since virgin births and disappearing bodies are not part of my religious reality, perhaps I should go to some other place which puts less strain on my credulity. There are other obstacles too, such as aspects of the present policies of the Church, and indeed all the religious establishments of which I disapprove. But on the other hand I know I have to go sooner or later because so far that's one of the regular places where I can focus on God and He becomes close. I can talk to Him there and in the silence give Him my attention, otherwise it withers. So as long as He fixes our appointments there, I have to go. I don't want to lose Him.

As I write this, I know I haven't been for a long time (about half a year) and there is a message for me in what I myself am writing as I am writing it. It is 'Get going, Blue! W.W., Smokey, your soul, your Granny's soul, your Guardian Angel, Jesus and Anne Frank want you.'

I want to wander into that uncluttered chapel again and wash myself in the silence and space. 'I'm a poor little lamb that has gone astray, ba ba ba.' I haven't plugged in for a long time – too long, and my thoughts show it. This is all very anthropomorphic but I can't change it.

Some Carmelites I got to know alive and dead

There was Father Nicholas who introduced me to Irish poetry, to Kavanagh, about peasants and their loyalty and bondage to their land and Irish national feeling. He tried to keep clear of the blinkered kind of nationalism for which I respected him. One could love one's own inheritance without it. I had, of course, the same problem with my own Jewish nationalism. I had to remind myself how much tragedy nationalism and tribalism had brought to Europe. I bought a book to teach myself Irish, but the phonetics and spelling made me dizzy. It was not a language I could pick up. I either settled down to learn or left well alone. Compared to it, Hebrew and even Aramaic were a doddle. But for Father Nicholas, I at least tried.

It was Father Nicholas who introduced me to Father Ross, one of the most beautiful people I have ever met, in body and soul. Too beautiful even for sexual thoughts. He was an Australian and had hunted sharks before becoming a contemplative. He was studying for a doctorate. He tried to explain the subject matter of it to me several times but it was too exalted for me to understand. I couldn't even make sense of its title, let alone its contents. I was too earthbound a spirit and he was too pure. But he was great fun.

And he did introduce me to 'holy picnics', at which he educated me in the three Carmelite teachers, Teresa, Thérèse and John. He was an exceptionally fine cook and it was a pleasure to consume his Spanish omelettes while I was pouring out cheap Spanish wine and willing my soul to burst into the inner regions of St Teresa's Inner Castle.

This didn't work out. The 'Inner Castle' seemed to show how you could work your way from the moat through various chambers until you attained the inner contemplative core. Provided you were conscientious, I thought it would yield results like those books on 'How to Learn Spanish' or 'Guitar Playing in Three Weeks'. But I couldn't make their spiritual equivalent work (if it was an equivalent). One moment, borne on a wave of illumination and insight, I was making steady progress through the inner halls, and the next moment I was dumped way outside the moat. It was rather like my driving test, which I took time after time, each time failing on something different. There was no logical reason to stop me taking the test for ever.

Father Ross was a romantic who breathed deep sincere breaths as he contemplated in the chapel silence. I shouldn't have been peeking but I was trying to get pointers on the inner life and he seemed to have a strong one. I wondered if I could ever have the same but spiritually we were not built the same way. Reluctantly I realized that in some matters I was more of a free-thinking Protestant Jew than a Catholic one. But I did learn from Ross what obedience meant and consistency. They weren't my virtues but I witnessed living proof of what they could accomplish in a devotee. He was a very pure person. I only use that adjective very sparingly.

I listened intently to the short sermons in the chapel. They were short, unaided by art or rhetoric, and they didn't put on the style. I had to strain to hear them, what with the assorted brogues and the quiet voices. They reminded me of Rabbi Leo Baeck's sermons when he was speaking for himself and not for a community or organization. He didn't sermonize for very long and he spoke so softly I had to strain to hear. They were true thoughts for the day!

There was a great deal of fondness for me among the fathers and brothers. Father Levinas I am sure prayed for me constantly. I could sense his affection and his prayers. Both mean a lot to me. They trusted me even when I invaded their quiet world with TV and radio, and I tried to honour their trust.

There was a spiritual charm about the whole set-up which impressed me when I first went to visit them, and it didn't wear off for me even after I got to know them better with their differences and disorders. When I first went to visit them they told me they were the novice house of their order. But they had no novices — I certainly couldn't see any! I was discourteous enough to point this out. They just sighed and said yes, it had been a long time since they had had any but God would or would not provide. It was such a refreshing antidote to the numbers game, ecclesiastical style, that I could have kissed them. This was the real contemplative McCoy!

But after an important Carmelite in London gave a shove, God did in fact provide with a most interesting mixed bag of novices who all seemed to descend on the house at once. I stayed friends with some who made it and the ones who went another way. I even wondered if I could become a novice without being a Christian. But even I could see this was too absurd. Still, it shows the attraction the place held for me. The poverty wouldn't have worried me. After the rat-race it would have been a relief. Perhaps I could have learned to cope with chastity, though that was pushing it because I was a normal active middle-aged chap without great powers of sublimation, but the obedience would have been my Waterloo. I also realized that visiting such a place for two or three days and tasting their goodies is very different from a whole lifetime of it.

I met a hermitess about the same time. I was given special permission to see her. Her call had come to her in a cinema in Bournemouth and wouldn't go away. 'How did you feel,' I asked her, 'when the bishop came and locked you in?' 'I burst into tears,' she replied, 'and said to myself "What have you done?" ' To my knowledge she's still enclosed. Another friend of mine has become a hermit in Jerusalem. It seems as good a response to a near hopeless situation as any.

I am going to the Carmelites again soon. I want to find out if it's still our (mine and Smokey's) meeting place, or must I move on? It takes two to tango, as I've said, so it's over to him.

Now, though Kim, my friend and partner at that time, was

not sympathetic to Catholicism, he did like my caravan of holy celibates – he was an honest chap. Faith in him had been frozen in his formation in public school. As for me, I shall be paying another visit to my Priory after finishing this book and handing in the manuscript to my publishers.

Anneliese's guru hunt

My friend Anneliese, who had built a religious conference centre and retreat house in Germany, was looking for someone to do a repair job on her own faith, which had started to come apart during the war.

Though middle-aged when I met her, she still had the eager innocence of a child, and I agreed to join her in a guru hunt, as I also liked salvation in different flavours.

One of the gurus said that God was dead, but most agreed He was alive and lived in them exclusively. Some of them said they lived in Him. Perhaps this was the same thing, and perhaps it wasn't. Anneliese and I couldn't figure it out. One lady told us she was God and asked for a double portion of Anneliese's chocolate pudding. Anneliese was a bit shirty about this but, after all, rank has its privileges.

Anneliese had read about a guru who knew God's telephone number, though when you rang it you got no reply. The guru said, 'What else do you expect?' Anneliese and I considered this remark over a bottle of Moselle and decided it wasn't unreasonable, and might be quite profound.

Anneliese eventually found a super spiritual teacher who didn't fancy himself as God, though he was, thank God, a gentleman. He wasn't only holy, but he was also polite. Well, she confiscated him immediately and, lured by her goodness and the prospect of endless meditation in comfy surroundings with good food and central heating, he drove us back to her retreat house. He was as eager as a puppy to bust into the beyond. So eager that as he sped along the autobahn he started to meditate on the names of God before we got there. There were, I think, about 99, but I didn't count, as he half-closed his eyes while reciting them and lifted his hands from the steering wheel in supplication. Anneliese had a direct religious experience, and I had never felt closer to eternity.

I agreed with Anneliese that her centre could do with more spiritual tone, and suggested a live-in hermit. I had forgotten how literal Anneliese could be in the German manner. When I came again I found she had filched a real hermit from a real monastery. She had constructed for him a purpose-built cell on a neighbouring alp and had also thoughtfully provided a large Alsatian. The hermit could love the dog and the faithful dog would protect him. Both seemed to me rather lonely on their eyrie and I suspect had had enough of each other. The dog had no vocation for a solitary life; and the nice plucky hermit, for all his spiritual horsepower, could have done, I thought, with a pint in a pub.

Eventually Anneliese settled back in the bosom of her own church, which I agreed was the best thing. Why did she ever go on a guru hunt, for she was such a competent, practical woman, such a brilliant fund-raiser? 'Because I feel guilty', she said. 'I should have ended up in a concentration camp and I didn't.' Still, she had built a refuge for women in distress, and a house for refugees. She aided the German refugees fleeing from their land in the East which had been occupied. She also sent food parcels to the Poles who were occupying it. She made a home for apprehensive Jews, starving students and forlorn Turkish guest-workers. She had been grilled by the Gestapo and had adopted 13 children without any money. She made Germany pure for me – she was my own Deutsche Yiddishe mamma, my buxom blessed Brunhilde, my loving Lorelei.

She died about the same time as Sister Louis, whom she liked and respected. I hope she now realizes what I always knew and tried to tell her: that all the faith she sought on earth was already quite safe inside her.

A dog who got above herself

I knew there was something wrong as soon as I entered the pub. Pretending not to notice, I took my glass to a corner, and waited to see what would happen.

They were indignant about my dog Re'ach. While I'd been away on a lecture tour, people said she had got above herself, and wanted watching. The lady pianist whispered to me, in between her Brahms and her bitter, that they were beginning to call her Bigboots, which didn't bode well for a bitch.

I was puzzled, because though Re'ach wasn't bright, she was not given to fantasy either. She was a matter-of-fact sort of dog, concerned with chocs, bones and her plastic ball. If she were human, she would have been happy with her hockey sticks.

Or would she? I decided to test out the situation myself, and returned to the pub later that evening with Re'ach trotting by my side.

As soon as we got through the door, Re'ach dismissed me with a dirty look, and bounded up to the bar. I caught the glances of the clientele as she placed her paws on the bar and barked for the barman. When he saw her, his face lit up, his jaw dropped, and while she gazed into his blue eyes, he gazed into her brown ones. Then Re'ach nibbled his ear to remind him love wasn't everything, and he dutifully brought out her bowl.

My jaw began to drop too as he poured into it a tot of sweet vermouth with a chaser of still lemon. 'I don't give her fizzy', he explained conspiratorially. 'It goes up her nose and she doesn't like it.'

One drinker said to another, 'It's just not natural.'

'Just trying to better herself, poor dear', said the besotted barman.

Now I began to understand why she kept moving her dog-food closer to the dining-room table and liked to lay her head on a pillow. She didn't want to be an underdog any longer. She wanted to be 'treated natural', like a human being.

'And why not?' I said to the people in the pub. Religious people too get above themselves, because they want to better themselves. She wants to be a bit human, and we want to be a bit divine – it's the same sort of thing and none of us ever make it. I must look as ridiculous as Re'ach, I thought, clasping my hands together, speaking to someone who doesn't seem to be there and demanding special foods like bits of blessed bread. Of course it seems strange because it's not natural when we want to get above ourselves – it's supernatural!

To pacify everybody, I told them about a prayer meeting where the cantor hadn't shown up. Who would take his place?

'Take my dog', said a congregant with pride. 'He's got a lovely delivery.' To the astonishment of some and the indignation of others, the dog came forward and, planting his paws on the lectern, barked for silence, and then softly growled the liturgy.

'Wonderful, wonderful! He should become a rabbi at least', they said to his owner as they congratulated him.

He shook his head sadly. 'You tell him, he's set on making it in the media!'

Falling in love with love

I found myself in a small boat, banging a tin tray with a mug in a cotton-wool fog, halfway across the North Sea. At such times I have a tendency to review my life and ask the Almighty why. I knew the reason, though: it was love. We had met, had shared a chicken sandwich, and now I was sandwiched between this world and the next.

'Love makes the world go round', and the world hereafter too. Falling in love with God can be very similar to falling in love with a human being. You bump into each other one day, or trip over each other. You meet at a boring formal occasion, like the wedding service of a distant relation – and suddenly you know you want to meet again. Or you realize with wonder that the old familiar God you met years ago in Sunday School classes is alive and attractive (not very different from the boy or girl next door in class B movies). Or you start off by having values and find one day that they are alive. You can speak to them, they can answer back, and you can be in love with them as well as love them. They acquire a human face.

If you are hooked, you start haunting the place where you first met. You want to go to that particular church or synagogue and no other. It takes time to realize that God is everywhere. For although we are formally monotheists, it is easier for us to think and act as dualists. To live and keep sane, we cannot take reality whole, we have to divide it up, though it shows as few seams as the robe of Jesus. It is more convenient for society if one says, this is completely forbidden, that is completely permitted, this worship of God is valid and that form He doesn't care for, that He is present in the liturgy but not in the loo. In Judaism God might be, is in fact, beyond the categories we have become accustomed to, but to go beyond them and try to find this unification of opposites is a danger-ous pastime. It has led to visions and orgies, insight and insan-ity, saintliness and beastliness. On the other hand, if the search is given up or never attempted, the result, as I have said, is practical dualism. This is less attractive, but an easier option if you have a fearful temperament. It leads to heresy hunts, appropriating God and a formalism which divides religious experience from actual experience.

Belonging as I do to a legal religion, where one age is ending and another scarcely beginning before our eyes, the second danger is as real for me as the first. It is not, however, easy to adjust to the exact mixture of adventure and boredom that is required. It is a comfort – though a cold one – to know that God's will is done either way – whether we get the proportions right or wrong.

In any case, God may be everywhere, but for you at the moment He is localized in a place or an institution. The service takes the place of a guitarist in a café or the cabaret in a night-club. At first it is nice to have all the accoutrements of romance around: soft lights, music, candles – what more could you want? Even the sermon might turn you on – in love anything can happen, certainly at the beginning.

There will be moments, of course, when you will want to be alone. This is as difficult in religion as it is in ordinary life. In Protestant churches the doors are firmly shut and you cannot ask the caretaker for the key – he will feel suspicious, and you will feel illicit. Catholic churches and synagogues may also be barred, because the more people drop in, the more the insurance they have to pay. (The Lord of Hosts is as imprisoned by His possessions as any suburban couple.) Some groups dedicated to silence, such as the Quakers, have a meditation room, but it is hard to find and feels empty like a pub outside normal hours. Curiously enough, the highest percentage of locked churches I have found is in Spain. Even the temples you do get into are not always suitable. Sometimes they are cathedrals, and having a private talk with God in them is like trying to have an intimate chat in a department store.

Sooner or later the crisis will come, and you will have to take Him (or Her) back to your place. It is difficult because the Holy One does not fit your furniture or your books. If you are a Jew you will have to rearrange your kitchen, for example. As in any love affair, you will have to make room for Him inside yourself as well, in your heart.

It is not easy sharing a kitchen with anybody, and it is even less easy sharing yourself with another being. After the first rapture, there is the adjustment period when you both have to learn to live together. It can be very irritating. He wants to go to Mass and you want to go sailing. You would like a ham rasher or a battery chicken, and He says He could not stand it. If the love and commitment are strong, you can overcome the gap and, like many couples, you will gradually get more alike, and one day you may fuse together.

Of course there will be rows. You can tell Him to get out of your life, and He will go. But after love has gone, you will feel so empty, you will call Him back. There is nothing like the pleasure of making up. It usually leads to a release of love. With a human being, it is consummated in bed, and with a divine being, in repentance. Lovers' quarrels are well known, and the pattern can be repeated many times. But take care! After one quarrel He may leave you. You will wait for His return, and for the normal reconciliation. But He has His own will and own thoughts, and He may not return. Then you will have to live with the emptiness like any forsaken lover, when the colour drains out of the world and a dimension of it is lost and love is a memory.

At this time in my life I started dropping into places where I could pray: synagogues, churches and temples. After some hesitation, I found myself talking to God, usually asking Him what I should do next. I did not go in for thanks or praise, because at that time I did not think I had much to give thanks for. Nor did I find myself asking for forgiveness. My life had been chaotic, and a lot of it was not my fault. Whether He forgave me was His own business; whether I forgave Him or myself was mine.

I also had to work out if our love was exclusive or not. Did the love of God rule out the other loves of my life? Was He in fact jealous? With some people it does not seem that the relationship is like that. I increasingly came to see Him not as a rival to other loves, but as part of them. I looked into someone else's face with love, and found Him present. He in fact showed me what love looks like – its true face.

Having said all this, I give the cautions you need after a religious experience. You might intend to embrace the universe, but you can end up just giving yourself a hug or admiring your own spirituality, or kissing your own ego.

A moment of truth

Sometimes, after prayer, you see a familiar object as if for the first time, and it seems perfect and right.

A bridge game clarified the cosmic situation for me. It was late at night at a party, a bridge party. I sat near the players and looked at their cards. There was a tension between two of them – a husband and wife – which puzzled me. He was trying to win, and the more he succeeded the more angry she became, though it was a hidden anger. I pieced the reasons together from their conversation. The man was playing against his employer. The more he won at the game of cards, the more he angered his employer and lost in the game of life and livelihood. He had focused his emotions and feelings, his success and failure, on two-dimensional cardboard, and it was real enough in a two-dimensional way. His wife had focused her emotions and feelings, her success and failure, on three-dimensional objects of metal and stone – freezers, cars and garages. But success in two-dimensional reality meant failure in three-dimensional reality, as she realized. He realized it too after a resounding slam. He looked at her in triumph. She looked at him with irritation, and he sagged as he readjusted to the realities of three-dimensional life and the triumph blew out of him.

I watched, and saw how the reality of the cards was enclosed within the more inclusive reality of life, and how the logic of one ran counter to the other. But the reality of life itself is enclosed within the greater reality of eternal life, and we can only dimly sense its meaning and its demands. Devices (or realities), like angels, are whispers we recognize, pointing to this profounder reality which encloses our own life as our worldly life encloses a game of bridge.

Damn!

I started to peer at her over the edge of my pulpit – though one shouldn't peep – because she looked so jolly uncomfortable. And as I took the service I occasionally looked up from my prayer book and stole a glance at her, because I was curious as to what would happen to her.

She was obviously not used to synagogues or to services, and this was her once-a-year social call on her Creator. I wondered why she had come at all. Perhaps to say memorial prayers for the religion of her grandparents who had died? Ancestor worship is always the last faith to crumble. Her dress was subdued but expensive. It was also very new, and she creaked! After two or three blessings there was a discreet wiggle and an adjustment of buckles and straps. She conscientiously tried to follow the square black Hebrew letters, but occasionally she looked up from her devotions in a puzzled way at the eternal light. What was she asking? Probably the same questions asked by saint or sinner alike: 'Is there anybody there? If so, what's in it for me?'

As she was not at her ease, little things started to go wrong. She dropped a hanky and nearly lost a shoe. The handbag was saved by a quick leap, which distracted me and made me lose my place, so the choir sang the wrong Amen. But she was not going to give up. In a high, precise voice, she implored God, polite but surprised, 'to quicken the dead', 'to rebuild the walls of Jerusalem' and 'to keep His faith with those who sleep in the dust'. Instinctively she removed a speck of it with a shaped fingernail.

How long, how long, O Lord, I wondered, could she continue in this unnatural state, wearing clothes unadapted to her body, saying things irrelevant to her interests and being anybody but herself?

The silent prayers made her feel worse – as they often do. A brooch came adrift. Then a glove. Then it was all too much. She slouched back defeated. Then I saw her lips move, and I knew she said 'Damn!' She had tried to do the right thing, but the more right it was supposed to be, the more wrong it felt.

I felt so happy for her then. For the first time she was herself, not a mask or a projection, or a nice person sucking up to the Almighty, or a conforming child, who knew which side her cosmic bread was buttered. And because she was herself, prayer was possible. In fact it had already taken place and been answered, though she didn't know it. Something inside her had wanted freedom, and lo and behold, her shell had cracked. Is not that a wonder?

Whether it brought her pleasure or pain, I don't know – religion brings both – but she had become real. We often confuse our ragbag of desires, our mental fluff, with the real prayer of our being, and we wonder why God hasn't paid more attention to our rubbish. Fortunately He is selective in what He listens to. 'Blessed are you Lord, who listens to prayer' – if the prayer is worth listening to, that is.

Look at the birdie!

Religious institutions often treat the Holy Spirit like a budgie. They coo at him, and want him to answer 'tweet-tweet'. They would like him to fly out of his cage and into their lives, just for a minute or two of course. But this bird won't move – he just seems to eye them distantly, birdily and beadily.

Then they say, 'He is an ungrateful beggar. Doesn't he realize there is a recession on, and lots of birds are homeless? Look at them all migrating to the North Pole or the Sahara, while birdie here has a nice ecclesiastical cage and central heating.'

I don't think the Spirit is like a budgie or even a dove, as he is usually depicted. He is a very strange bird indeed, and wilier than we thought. He is, in fact, much like God on Mount Sinai. 'I will be gracious to whom I will be gracious, and show mercy to whom I will show mercy.' Beat that for wilfulness!

But when the bird has flown, how do we get him back into our lives? For this bird means freedom and soaring, and without his wings there is no life in the universe, no heady love. Getting the Spirit back into our lives is like luring a rare bird into our gardens.

Firstly, be quite clear that you are not going to cage him, because caging free creatures is nasty, and in this case quite useless. But put on protective clothing, because the Spirit can lead you into strange places, to condemned prisoners in their cells, and into the wilderness. He has done that before, you know.

You can, of course, put out little pious titbits for him, juicy prayers that you have cooked up on your own. But he is so capricious. You never know what he is going to accept. It was said, 'The wind bloweth where it listeth . . . but thou canst not tell whence it cometh and whither it goeth: so is every one that is born of the Spirit.' Too true, too true, so blow you and your bribes.

There is only one way to get him that I know, and that is to stalk him – but very gently. This is how you do it. Pretend to be like him, imitate his ways, and all you know of his habits. Pretend you are flying. Don't just be ethical, be good! Do foolish and generous things for people. Don't hit them with your clumsy old fists! Touch them as softly and gently as if you had the wings of a dove – not those great hairy arms.

If you are that gentle, birdie gets interested and confused, you know. He thinks perhaps you aren't the clumsy ape you seem, but a soaring, gentle, wild bird, like himself. If you want to have the Spirit, pray to be like the Spirit, pray that you are so like the Spirit that no one, not even the Spirit, can tell you apart.

'Coo-oo, tweet-tweet. Good luck!'

Gender lessons of travel

We were finally slotted into our seats in the package plane and I warily inspected the man and woman in my row. In our adequate but restricted *Lebensraum*, for the few hours of the flight, we were going to be more intimate than we wanted because I had a prostate problem and they were between me and the washroom. But the holiday was already elating me, transforming and purifying me. The bad vibes were fading and I was feeling more and more benign. I no longer had to deal with people or put them on committees or think up the tactful wise words they wanted of me as their minister. I needed no longer to flinch from them because they were problems but could at last look at them as people. I could listen to them. If I only turned slightly I could 'people-watch' them.

And 'people-watch' can easily become 'God-watch', I told myself excusingly – because I had thought of meditating or praying on the plane like some pious Anglo-Catholics I knew who always scampered away from life to liturgy if they got the chance. 'If I purified my motives and didn't do people-watch to make fun of my fellow travellers (though our fellow humans are indeed funny – like us), or to annoy them or to feel superior to them,' I told myself, 'my people-watch could become a godly exercise.' For many of us, the closest we ever come to God is spotting Him in other people. It helps us to go on to the next lesson and spot Him inside ourselves.

The man and woman in my row had already made contact while I was contorting myself into reasonable comfort and debating my phoney spiritual problem. They had done it quickly, but then they were singles, and singles need someone more urgently than couples. Few of us feel complete alone. They were nice but preoccupied, especially the young man. He was already recounting with restricted gestures the heroic story of his own struggle against life's unfairness. As I've told the same tale many times myself, I was more interested in the girl beside him and how she managed to consume a burger and bun from her bag, while nodding in sympathy and skilfully throwing in 'oh's, 'ah's and 'really's between bites. Listening and eating like that was an art, and she didn't drop a crumb. She must have raced to the airport without time for breakfast, but of that she never said a word.

I suddenly wondered how it felt being a woman and being expected to listen to men. Do they listen because they want to? Or is it their nature? Or the way we programme them as babies? And my mind roamed further to the parts never mentioned in sermons. What was it like having periods? And don't they ever want to reverse roles and gesticulate too and talk about themselves non-stop while a man smiles in sympathy and tut-tuts? And how did they feel when they saw all those conferences on the TV conducted by macho males locking their horns like elks while the women had to clear up the mess? Did women hunger for men sexually as men hungered after them? Did they have the same fantasies about each other? What did women really think of men?

Not much, according to my late mother and aunt. In the retirement home where my friend and I used to visit them in the last year of their lives, we noticed how much they talked about meeting their mother, great aunt and sister in heaven, but seemed surprised when we pointed out that their father and husbands would await them too. They didn't mind but men just seemed unreal.

I suddenly realized that though I've been concerned with marriage guidance, divorce and family matters all my working life, I've never really known what it's like to think as a woman in a woman's body. And the opposite is probably true too. Do women understand the expectations of power and success most males have to carry? They can't hide their tiredness with false orgasms – their lack of erection gives them away. Perhaps we all ought to go to evening classes and learn about each other, and I don't mean just sex but gender.

The text 'male and female created He them' (Genesis 1.27) came into my mind. On this holiday I would try to understand more and judge less. This would help me understand myself because the text should really be read 'male and female created He us'.

My meditation was interrupted as the little hot lunch trays were distributed. The man, I was pleased to note, offered the woman a little bottle of wine to accompany it, which she tactfully refused. But after he had drunk his wine, when he was beginning to mellow and untense, he began to ask the woman beside him at which hotel she was staying and what she did back home, and whether she had the same problems in her office as he did in his, which was magnanimous of him. 'Oh, my work isn't so interesting', she said casually and tactfully, and he must have approved because he then invited her to his hotel barbecue. She had won the set and I noticed a speculative look in her eye as she gazed at him in between more 'oh's, 'ah's and 'really's.

Penny plain or tuppence coloured?

One hour of repentance and good deeds in this world is better than all the life of the world to come; and one hour of calmness of spirit in the world to come is better than all the life of this world.

(Sayings of the Fathers, Ch. 4 v. 22)

The basic problem with religion is not a romantic one, just a crude and simple one, and I did not learn it from any guru whom I had to chase up in some inconvenient cave in the Himalayas, but right at home, from my dog Re'ach. Readers of the Bible should not be surprised by this animal intrusion, because though dogs and horses get a bad press there (eating up Jezebel, obstinacy and lust), animals make good prophets as well as pets.

Indeed, the opening lines of the Hebrew liturgy at Jewish services were not first spoken by a Jew, but by Balaam the Jew-hater and, even more surprisingly, his mentor was an ass. The word of God is mediated to us through many messengers. It is only our snobbism which prevents us receiving it. I learned a lot about religion from my dog Re'ach. You always do from any being you love.

This was how I learned it. Whenever I left my house, my dog Re'ach would look at me mournfully and reproachfully from the stairs – the tragic look on her face reminded me of Bette Davis, registering sorrow and passion in *Now Voyager*, a film which had moved me profoundly in my youth. Re'ach, was a very Jewish dog. No wonder dogs were not favoured by the prophets, they were so much better at inducing guilt.

Whenever I came back, the reverse would take place. As I opened the door, Re'ach turned, amazed, towards it. Now, dogs can't laugh but they can show astonishment. Re'ach being a Jewish dog, showed it in a big way. She leapt down the stairs, woofing and baying, and then brought me down in an amorous tackle. Standing on my chest, she would lick me triumphantly and ecstatically, like a canine Orpheus whose Eurydice was on reprieve.

This drama took place whether I had been on a long visit to North America or on a short errand to the newspaper man round the corner. Eventually wearying of this dramatic life, I went to consult my vet. 'Doesn't she learn from experience?' I complained. 'Is she so dumb that she never realizes I'll come back, or does she like emotional orgies?'

Patiently he explained my dog to me. 'Being an animal,' he said, 'and very attached to you, she can't help these great disturbances.' 'You see,' he added, 'people and things are real for her when they are within the range of her senses. When she can see you, touch you, smell you (smelling is the most important), you are alive. When you move outside the range of her senses, it is as if you were dead. Now you can understand her a bit better. How would you feel if someone you loved died and was resurrected every weekend and twice on most weekdays?' I paused to consider my life under such circumstances and agreed weakly that it would certainly be rocky.

Now, according to the psalms, we are a little higher than animals, and just a little lower than the angels. No wonder religion is tough in such an in-between situation. Because we are a little lower than the angels, we are able to accept the reality of a being and a world we can't sense – but only just! The kingdom of heaven is not a foreign country to us and we know it is not fairyland. But our hold on it is very weak, because we are only a little higher than the animals, not very far from my poor dog Re'ach. In fact we humans have the same difficulty of ascribing life to a *mysterium tremendum*, as she has in ascribing it to me when I am absent. Like her, what is not sensed quickly becomes nonsense for us.

When we deal with spiritual matters, we are working at the limit of our perception – finite animals reaching out to infinity.

I think it is more difficult for me to hold on to the intangible now than it was when I first dropped into the Quaker meeting so many years ago at Oxford. Advertising has got slicker and there is more of it. It has persuaded me that I need a lot more things – not that I needed much persuading. In the early 1950s, for example, men were only permitted a slick of brilliantine. Deodorants were finickety, and bath salts pansy. We must have smelt rather gamey, but we were not aware of it. Now I pack my pre-shave, after-shave and splash-on, even when I am off to an ascetic retreat.

Like most people, I have got happiness and comfort well and truly muddled. Each year I look through the tourist bro-chures, and buy myself a chunk of escapism on a costa because the pictures assure me (though the print is reticent) that happiness will come too, as a bonus extra, like those old trading stamps we used to get handed to us. (They looked so grand and were worth so little.) And yet I know that it never works out like that. Happiness, like the kingdom of heaven, is within me. Yes, I would prefer to be unhappy in comfort than in discomfort, but I have been very happy in a boarding house, and suicidal in a deluxe hotel. Comfort means objects, but happiness is of the spirit. It's a truth so easy to state and so difficult to live.

This sounds so spiritual that I suspect it. It slips down too easily, like cheap romances. Being an in-between person I have to do justice to the realities in which I live and have my being. Spirituality can be trusted only if it can deal sanely, sensibly and helpfully with its twin, the material world. It's no use loving people's souls if you are disgusted by their liver and lights. The material world is the testing ground of all spirituality.

A lot of it fails the test. A lot of spirituality (especially, for some reason, if it is in French) sounds very inspiring. But then as you are reading it on the top of a crowded bus, you can't help asking yourself, 'Now what did all that mean?' And a dreadful suspicion forms in your mind. 'Did it mean anything at all?'

I don't think we can be sure, unless our spirituality is accompanied by an attestation from the material world. I have never ceased to brood over the strange portion of the Pentateuch I had to read at my confirmation – my Bar Mitzvah, at which I 'became a man'. On thinking it over, the guts and gore of the sacrifices came from my ancestors' possessions and they didn't have many, only their animals. When these went up in smoke on the altar, so did their shares and building society accounts and pension funds. The guts were crude,

135

but they made their sin offerings and guilt offerings real, and validated them.

I sat in a reserved seat in a crowded train. I had reserved it because I needed to read a book on spirituality. It was hot stuff and, as I read it, God seemed to come very close to me. So did a noisy lady standing in the gangway. The book seemed to tell me quite clearly that the reality of God is more important than any experience of Him. Reluctantly obedient, and thoroughly annoyed, I closed the book and gave up my seat. It was my sacrifice. Unless I had made it, I could never have opened that book again.

The experience of God came a lot at the start of my dive into religion, and I hope I will get a dollop of it at the end to ease my entry into eternity. But in the meantime I have had to make do with the reality of God. (It's not always God I've prayed for, but success or ease or evasion which I've dressed up in divinity. No wonder such prayers were never answered.)

Some friendships of many years were coming to an end. Before, we had all helped each other, now it didn't work out like that. There was the usual froth of self-justification which marks all changes in direction, with their accompanying insecurities (I said . . . you said . . . he said . . . she said . . .), the whining, the trivial points of honour, the secret scoreboard of hidden hurts. As the instincts launched me into this tedious and selfish exercise, I prayed . . . not to get my way, or to score, or even to patch things up, but to give up with affection and if possible with love. And the presence of God seemed to move into the faces of my friends, and well . . . we still speak occasionally and we may help each other again, though in a different way, God willing. That's all, and that's religion . . .

when you face a blank wall, faith is knowing that there is a door, if it is a door you want and pray for. The experience of St John of the Cross is relevant in a suburban parlour.

This 'failure' concealed a 'success', which concealed a hidden danger. To cheer myself up in the empty evenings which followed, coming home to a room in which the washing up I left in the morning remained exactly as I had left it, I called on God to enlighten me. He preferred to lighten me instead. As I have said before, I had always expected religion to make me heavy, but in fact it gave me back once again both love and laughter, as it had done in the Quaker meeting house in Oxford.

Jokes and humour burst into my prayers. I dispensed this mixture over the radio, and found it had the same effect on others as it had on me. To my astonishment, I became a celebrity (third class, after Arthur Scargill and Norman Tebbit). I never thought the rewards of the Spirit would be like this, and decided to take another look at the last verses of Job, and their suburban happy ending – the ones that many spiritual people get snooty about.

Although spirituality is see-through, without it the real world goes wrong very easily. If you are over-preoccupied with sex, you can become very trivial; if you are mastered by your 'image', you become phoney to yourself. My own experience has taught me that the pieties of religion are not commands but functional necessities of life – not cake but bread, ordinary bread – absolutely necessary for my self-respect.

It pleases me that God has become ordinary to me. He (or She – I have to learn to adjust) is no longer an exotic experience, bedecked with the tinsel jewellery of the imagination. In fact I don't get worried if I don't experience Him at all. For the reality of God makes the experience of Him a toy. This reality is enough with its silences, its doubts and the busy business of religion. God is as much in them as He was in the previous Technicolor episodes, but I have to learn what is being said to me through the obvious.

For what is this reality which endures when the imagination gets tired and goes to sleep? It is being nice to other people, trying to love them and, if you can't, at least not hating them, passing plates at parties, helping them with their luggage, telling them the time without making a fuss, letting yourself be used without becoming a doormat, and keeping your integrity in a tricky time.

Now I hear you say 'Rabbi Blue, what dull stuff! Why, it's the kind of thing people teach in any old-fashioned Sunday School.' And I answer a bit ruefully, 'Yes, you're right, it is. The only difference is that once I tried to teach it to children, now as an adult I try to practise it myself.' It seems an awfully long journey to rediscover my own platitudes. But at last I know their heights and depths.

And I can hear Him cackling His head off!

To have your bone and eat it

My dog Re'ach was a serious, contented animal who had a purpose in life. This purpose was centred on a lump of plastic, shaped and coloured to resemble a bloody beef chop, which squeaked when she bit it.

On summer mornings she waited impatiently until she could clock in at Kensington Gardens and get down to work. The gardens were thick with courting couples who lay prone, plastered together with dreamy desire. This my dog Re'ach was determined to destroy.

Bending over a girl who was sodden with sleep and love, she squeaked her chop. The girl, looking up, would see a black muzzle, a yard of wicked red tongue, and the bloody chop. Not unnaturally, she screamed. This aroused her swain from his deep dream of peace, and he would curse and Re'ach would squeak her chop defiantly until he rose up in wrath and Re'ach scampered away, well pleased with herself – another vigilante mission successfully accomplished, and not without danger.

This pastoral idyll could have gone on all summer, with the screams of girls and the squeak of chops, the oaths of swains and the woofs of dogs, as regular as the dawn chorus, a sort of silly pastoral symphony.

But in any Garden of Eden, a serpent lurks to rear its head. My American friend didn't look like a serpent. He was chubby and genial and, like many elderly Americans, generous to a fault. Re'ach struck him as 'kinda cute', and as he was partial to chocolate chip ice cream and sweet Martini, which Re'ach kinda liked too, '*leur sublime s'amalgama*' – they shared the same ideal – as Saint-Simon so acutely observes of Archbishop Fénelon and Madame Guyon, his mystic guide.

To increase her contentment, though contentment is content with itself and needs no increase, as my American friend should have known, he presented pooch with a plastic squealing bone to complement her squeaking chop. Re'ach gazed at the bone besotted, and when she bit it and found out it squealed, she ran around the garden again and again, intoxicated by the quantity and the quality of her possessions.

She squeaked her chop but then had to let it go to pick up her bone. She then squealed her bone and let it go to pick up her chop. Neither action felt right for she wanted both, and she made a frantic attempt to hold both her chop and her bone at the same time but her jaws, alas, could not cope.

Her contentment had gone. When she held one, the memory of the other would surface in the murk of her mind, and her grief over what she did not have spoilt the pleasure of what she did. It was an existential problem, as Sartre could have told her and Simone de Beauvoir too. But Re'ach was not a philosophical dog, so she sat back on her haunches and howled at the tragedy of life. It was too much.

I thought of her as I sat in the synagogue. The rabbi was chanting the Scriptures from the scroll and the words were uncompromising: 'See I have set before you this day life and good, and death and evil ... Choose life.... (Deut. Ch. 30, v. 15 e. 19).

Now, Re'ach would not have liked that. She wanted to have her bone and eat it. And sometimes when I think of all that has to be given up for the sake of eternal life, I don't like it either. And I too would like to sit back on my haunches and howl.

Marrow with a message

When I wake up, I hate listening to the news – there is so much sour anger around. It's justified anger of course, so they tell us, but it has a rancid taste and it stops me jumping out of bed. I pull my duvet back over my head instead.

And wherever you go, the scenario is the same dreary stuff, whether it's in Lebanon, Northern Ireland, Yorkshire or India. One side clenches its teeth and shouts 'wogga, wogga, wogga' and then the other side snarls back 'wagga, wagga, wagga', and then after a few bleats and baas from the high-minded, both sides settle down to a bottle session – throwing them unfortunately, not drinking from them. And with the bottles they throw all these dear old tribal bygones, hurled since time immemorial: bricks and bottles to warm things up, followed by the hard stuff – bullets and bombs.

To get some relief, I switch off the radio and start brooding over my own domestic problem, which at the moment happens to be an enormous intractable marrow left over from the harvest festivals. The trouble is I don't need a marrow; I need a message with a moral which I can turn into a sermon. There should be a message in my marrow, because it was grown in a monastery and given to me by a monk, but it eludes me and this makes me angry – though not enough to throw a bottle.

It is a very big marrow and a very firm one – so firm, in fact, that none of us at home can cut or stuff it. We stabbed it with carving knives and sawed it with bread knives, and have drawn blood – our own – while the bloody marrow (I speak factually, not pejoratively) sits secure and smug in its skin.

But I have a clever friend called Pauline who finally took it on, because she makes models and sculpts, and she intends to bore a hole in it and throw out the pips. Then she is going to fill the hole, she says, with dark brown sugar and a pinch of ginger, and punch another hole in its bottom and then hang it up in an old pair of tights – washed, of course. The fermented marrow juice or liqueur will then drip through her tights into a suitable bottle, and one day we shall get merry on marrow, she says.

I have not made this recipe. I can merely describe it, as I just do not know what will happen, for another monk assured me that in his monastery a marrow exploded when it was treated in this way. They kept on renewing the sugar, he said, but you can have too much renewal. The smell of their marrow was so strong it blotted out the odour of their sanctity.

Now, I suppose there are some moral messages I can squeeze out of the marrow, though they are not as exciting as its juice.

I could say that from sweetness is distilled the liquor of life. I could also say that if you don't treat God's creation with respect, it will blow up in your face. But neither of these turns me on, and I can't deduce anything from a pair of washed tights.

But I've got a glimmering of an idea about how to use an

exploding marrow. It could be just the job for demonstrations. It wouldn't be lethal like bullets, or as dull as old bricks, and when people saw it flying through the air in a pair of tights they might learn to laugh again and recover their humanity.

I think that's what people need now: not another rehash of anger, whatever theology or ideology it's packaged in, but something new, something unexpected like an exploding marrow – something fresh which comes as a nice surprise, like the manna which dropped from heaven in the wilderness, or a strange star that rose in the east.

The bird at Christmas

Being a Jewish guest at a Christmas house party, I decide to do the Christian thing and offer to wash up. So on the morning after the night before, I'll descend at dawn in my threadbare bathrobe and languidly slosh dishes through tepid water, which I enjoy because over the sink I think, 'No more bubbly or bird, however delicious! Just Marmite toast with scalding tea from now on, please!' Though there's little chance of that, for after Christmas and Jewish Chanukah comes secular New Year, with more presents and vegetarian haggis sodden in whisky. I retch!

I've no longer got the stamina for non-stop partying, so this New Year's got to be different. Let's start, if we dare, by also giving some presents which cost nothing, given not from what we have but from what we are. A small change compared to climate change but it points us in the right direction. Now, this year I've received lovely things, but what I need most from my hosts is a slice of their Quaker silence. Let's be friends at an impromptu Quaker meeting around the tea table before we disperse. The Holy Spirit might speak in us and launch us into a good year. A compliment is a great gift – a perceptive and helpful one. 'O Rabbi Blue, your lovely legs are just right for a kilt.' Was my female fellow patient dotty or divine? I savoured her words often at night in hospital. Thank you, ma'am.

A handwritten recipe makes a good present too – provided you haven't left out vital stages. So does a promissory note to clean your kitchen oven. Or listen for an hour to your woes. Or comfort a bereaved oldie at the bar.

Don't worry if your present is rejected or misunderstood. Say you've given sandwiches to street people with greetings and they've given you the brush-off. Remember they've been rejected so often, they need to reject someone themselves. Offer your humiliation to God. It's the only pressie possible. He's got everything else.

And as for being misunderstood. Well, Sammy brings his poor old mother from Siberia to London and installs her in Mayfair luxury where she's desperately lonely. So he sends her a rare, expensive, Siberian-speaking parrot for company and a few days later rings anxiously. 'You're a wonderful son, Sammy', she said. 'Poor people like me don't get such presents in Siberia. So tasty!' she sobbed, licking her lips, while Sammy keeled over in shock. Treat yourself to a different New Year, dears!

The Gay Gordons

I hadn't danced for years. Not since the 1960s. I remember exactly when I stopped. It was in the 1960s. In the middle of a dance on holiday, my partner suddenly unhooked herself from me and started doing her own thing. Feeling a fool trying to dance on my own, I retired to my seat in a huff and never took to the floor again, until, that is, when I whooped, yelled and pranced in the Gay Gordons.

This came about on another holiday, a working one. Like many professionals, I sometimes try to combine a holiday with a conference. I give a lecture and they provide my fare and stay. Some of you will exclaim at my luck but combining them isn't easy. Sometimes there's not much holiday to it and you're conducting a problem clinic far into the night.

The friendliest one I ever went to (and the most pious) took place in Scotland. That's when I dared to dance the Gay Gordons because I was so relaxed. The university where it took place was reassuring. The halls of residence were full of fellow oldies like me, filling the holidays of their sunset years with folk dancing, origami and Mary Queen of Scots. Americans with Jacobite pretensions pored over tartans, and pleasant

Japanese photographed me, each other, each other and me, and each other and every sporran in sight.

At breakfast we compared the conferences we were attending. A transatlantic lady who, like me, was into oatcakes slathered with Dundee marmalade, asked, 'Are you researching clan tartans?' 'No,' I replied through a mouthful of my marmalade, 'I'm at a conference for lesbians and gays.' She stopped masticating, mid-mouthful. 'Well, what do you know!' she muttered.

To reassure her we were no lewd lot, I added, 'They're all Catholics, very pious and prayerful.' 'What, real Romans?' she exclaimed. 'Oh yes,' I answered proudly 'cradle Catholics too, not just converts! Why, we've even got two priests and a nun.' She digested this information along with another oatcake. 'Are you a friar or something?' she said, probably because I looked too dishevelled for solemn monk status. 'A something,' I said, 'a Reformed Jewish rabbi.' She clapped her hands and exclaimed delightedly that that's what she loved about holidays. You never knew what surprises you would experience on them or who you would meet. Well, now she had heard and seen it all.

But she hadn't really! She should have seen our conference at the ceilidh, with our lads in their kilts, frills and dirks and our lasses in sashes and trews, kicking up their heels in the Gay Gordons. It was the first time I'd danced for years, as I've said, and I'd rarely felt so at home and happy. Two clansmen assured me I could wear a kilt too – my surname really existed in a subclan or sept. They also said I had the right rump. Oh those Scots! A little economical with the truth maybe but how courteous *quand même*!

My breakfast friend interrupted these reminiscences by suddenly asking me, 'So what do you get out of it, rabbi, seeing you don't even share the same scriptures?'

She was right. But all gays have a problem combining the truths of tradition with the truths of their own experience. Some gays are bitter and short-circuit the problem saying, 'Since my faith has no place for me, I've no place for it!' and never go to church or synagogue again. But the people I met were following the harder path by piecing together the public scriptures from the past and the private scriptures of their own lives.

The latter are sort of scriptures, too, because God didn't stop speaking at some date in the past but continues His work in us, refining His revelation. That's how slavery was not merely ameliorated but abolished, and women have not only acquired status but are now also moving on towards equality. God's continuing revelation has stopped us torturing old women as witches, permitted us interest on our building society accounts, taught us to respect other faiths, not fight them, and it's why majorities no longer burn minorities, theological and sexual, but tolerate them, even if they don't yet accept them.

I was pleased I had worked it out and turned to enlighten her. But I had been pondering in silence too long and she had gone to hit today's Whisky Trail. But the Japanese were still there. One of them asked me politely why Englishmen like me oppressed the Scots, denying them their freedom. Through the window I pointed to some brawny, kilted chaps bounding up Arthur's Seat. And I replied equally politely that any such subjugation would be most imprudent from a puny, pusillanimous southern Britisher like me, of the Mosaic persuasion.

While he looked up these exciting new words in his upside-down dictionary, I blessed God for freeing me from my ghetto. I had begun to think of the world as one big Jewish problem, and in the Scottish fresh air realized again a truth I'd almost forgotten, that more basic even than being Jewish or English was being a human being. My transatlantic friend was right. 'You never knew the surprises you would experience on holiday.'

She was so right. I felt exhilarated by my fresh freedom. And that's how I came to whoop and yell in the Gay Gordons that night.

Strange holiday – the real thing!

The loveliest holiday I ever had was in hospital, and not an expensive private one but an ordinary NHS one. I don't know how I got into it, though when I came to, the nurses told me I had had a fit outside a joke shop – a full-scale epileptic one, grand mal. I had gone rigid and purple like an aubergine and then crashed my head against the kerb stone. This may sound horrific but fits are a spectator sport and I was unconscious of it until I came to and the doctors were doing tapestry work on my skull.

They advised me to stay in over the bank holiday and I wasn't going to protest because the rest of my life was not going that well (hence the fit) and I badly needed a holiday from responsibility and from myself.

Most of the doctors were away over that weekend and there were few admissions, so an atmosphere of peace descended on the wards. I had no visitors, my friends were either away or had not heard, and I had no desire to tell anyone where I was or what had happened and cope with their concern. I was content in the company of the other patients in my half-empty ward. I enjoyed the anonymity of worn regulation nighties, and the absence of fuss.

We lay torpid like the bodies on a costa, occasionally offering each other sweets or advance warning of the tea trolley. Some were quite ill, far worse than me, and I was touched by how nice they were to me and each other. I had expected their problems would make them tetchy and difficult, but it was the opposite. Their problems had brought out their original goodness and I found myself blessing God for the care in them. We all knew the score about each other and were tactful about it.

One instance. I had come in without the normal toiletries, books or bags. They shared their Indian savouries with me and gave me squirts of aftershave and even offered to let me borrow their glasses because mine had got smashed when I fell.

The days of that weekend passed like a dream, reading the magazines you find in dentists' waiting-rooms, gazing at London town distanced by the thick glass of the windows, with all its restlessness and passion softened.

At first I mused about the might-have-beens of my life and then fantasized about what would have happened if I had chosen differently. These fantasies then came together in stories, and effortlessly the plan of my first novel (as yet unfinished) formed in my mind.

I realized I was not particularly attached to this life. It had its moments but I had experienced too much depression and anxiety with them to want it to last for ever. At some time I would be willing to call it a day because I had gone through it, I had done it and was curious as to what lay on the other side, if it had another side.

I managed to wander down to the hospital chapel where

I just sat and invoked Whomsoever Whatever, and waited patiently for whatever happened or didn't. It had a good atmosphere because it was continually sanctified by the prayers of those who meant business and weren't just repeating words. So its quietness was no emptiness.

Like many patients, I thought the nurses were angels. I certainly didn't encounter a grumpy or vindictive one. When the doctors returned and the bank holiday was over, I realized the weekend had given me all that I had ever wanted from a holiday, without frenetics or overstrain. I said this to a nurse who at first said she was astonished but then admitted that the calmness of such weekends touched her also.

After my partner and I broke up, I went on a commercial holiday to recover. The sun and the pool were satisfactory. It cost a lot and was not nearly as satisfying as the hospital. There I had moved a step nearer eternity and I liked it. It was an adventure.

Thinking spiritually about holidays, I realized how often we recreate the same tensions, the same situations, the same dramas that we are trying to escape from back home. It is the same with synagogues and churches. Lots of tired businessmen join them as an antidote to the competitions and combative materialism of their working lives. But as soon as they get to church or synagogue, they are unable to break the pattern, the compulsion, and throw themselves into fundraising drives, constitutional subcommittees and competition for office. They recreate the very world they were trying to escape. And it is the same with ordinary holidays too.

During my hospital 'holiday' I found the answer to problems, not just their repetition. I tried telling people this but they didn't believe me and thought it was just the tail end of my fit. But thank you, NHS, you touched me with the truth that had almost passed my understanding. I had needed my fit to know it.

My friend Fred

My friend Fred stared up in awe at the skyline of the small
Spanish town. It was punctuated by towers, turrets, crosses and
crowns like the quills of a porcupine. Church façades reared up
around us crowded with sad stony saints, which looked as if
they had been carved out of Common Market butter, their
girdles and gridirons frozen in a high baroque breeze.

I like my religion penny-plain, but Fred likes his tuppence
coloured. 'There'll be nice nooks and niches in them,' said
Fred, 'with saints and such.'

'I prefer lights,' I said, 'to focus my faith. Eternal lights,
candle lights, I don't mind, provided they're not electric.'

'Would you care to pray with me, Lionel?' said Fred.

'I don't mind if I do', I replied. 'Though services don't
switch me on, I'm partial to prayer.'

But our assault on the supernatural was foiled because all the
church doors were bolted. 'It's a liturgical lock-out', said Fred
gloomily and went off to find a cooperative cleric.

'We've got to find Sid', he said when he returned.

'You mean El Cid', I said, knowledgeably.

'I don't know his initial, Lionel,' said Fred humbly, 'but you
knock at the side door and ask for Sid the sacristan!'

But Sid, L. or otherwise, must have been locked in the sanctuary because he could not be found. Passing clergymen said the lock-out was the fault of the socialists, the capitalists, General Franco, long lunch hours and high insurance premiums. Nothing could be done about it. *Nunca, nunca!* – never, never!

At the tourist office they tut-tutted and suggested another sort of spirit – less holy, more helpful. The sherry shops were always open whatever the time. *Siempre, siempre!* – ever, ever! No trouble!

They were right, there was lots of room at the inn. The way to the wineries was wide and the waiters welcoming. First they showed us how to make the stuff, then they sat us down to drink it – chin chin, bottoms up, on the house.

'I'm shorry about your shaints', I said to Fred.

'Don't give it another thought, old chap', said Fred. Then, looking up at the lights shining from the bottles in the bar, he said, 'Lionel, can't you focus your faith on those?'

I glanced up at the glinting bottles, promptly invoked God's presence, and experienced some minutes of deep peace and piety.

'You'll never lack lights now,' said Fred contentedly, 'because when places of worship shut, the pubs start to open.'

I returned from holiday to my office. I was debilitated by dieting away those hotel meals and irritated by the pile-up of post. A visitor came to see me unexpectedly and I hardened my heart and, whatever the reason, that's a sin. Now, if there had been an eternal light on my filing cabinets or even a glinting bottle to focus my faith, it might have made all the difference. But there wasn't, and I realized it's not enough to look at a light in a synagogue or even in a bar, you have to carry your light inside you.

Barbecues and babies

Summer is a-coming in and suburbia celebrates Texan-style with blazing barbecues, fired by charcoal briquettes. 'It's all happening', says my mother excitedly, and bullies me into taking her along.

'Smoke gets in your eyes', as the lovely old song says. So docs a chip off the old charcoal. I can't converse, so while my mother socializes, I sit in sullen meditation with one eye closed and the other rimmed with red.

But you need both eyes about you at a barbecue. You can tell by feel which side your baguette is buttered, but you need your eyes to know which side of your chop is burnt and which is bloody.

With one eye, I see a cook has set fire to his pinny. I hear his squeals but feel no sympathy, for there is a whiff of meths from the meal. Next time I shall bring a compass to tell me which way the wind blows.

It is, alas, blowing my way now, reeking of sausage fat. But there is a recession, so they can only set cheap chipolatas alight, not whole oxen or heifers. I suddenly wonder what the animal sacrifices were like, that the Bible describes in the Sinai desert – I think of all that gore in all that heat and I shudder.

But I admire the ancient Hebrews. They were refugees like the Kurds and Somalis now, and destitute like some Bangladeshis, and the animals they sacrificed were their only wealth. They knew what we moderns don't want to know – that religion isn't real without sacrifice. Could I watch my savings go up in smoke? I doubt it.

Now, this touches my sore spot. I saw a picture in a paper of a starving kid you could keep alive for a few pounds. I feel manipulated but I can't get it out of my mind. I have to give to keep my religious self-respect.

But how much? How long is a piece of string? I know I'm not going to give everything to the poor – but nor are you.

One day by a miracle I might, but I wouldn't bank on it. I think back again to the Bible, for a rabbi said God didn't give His revelation to angels. It was meant for fallible human beings like us. So why not give the tithe of my income, commanded in that revelation, to charity? It may make the problem manageable, helping the starving Third World babies, and me.

Ten per cent net isn't heroic but if you're no saint like me, yet still have a conscience, there's a lot to recommend it – it's biblically based and practical, provided you keep it up.

One of my hosts interrupts my meditation to offer me more burnt flesh. I politely decline. When I get home, after I've sent my cheque, I shall reward my modest contribution to charity with a modest nut cutlet, cooked medium rare. With baked beans and brown sauce, it's yummy.

The Talmud wisely says, 'Just because you can't finish the job, isn't an excuse for not doing something about it.'

Home call

I sat in a café not far from the BBC and remembered my dog Re'ach, a big black animal, straightforward and sporty, who would have been happy in a Roedean hockey team. When I let her off the lead in the park, she rose in the air like Pavlova and raced exultant, round and round the green, chasing phantom rabbits, and panicking the lovers who lurked among the buttercups.

Then, one smiling day in July, when the sky was blue and families were unpacking their lunch, something happened. I let her off the lead and Re'ach did her usual entrechats. Then she ran a few steps, stood still in muzzy thought, and snorted. A yard of pink tongue hung foolishly from her mouth. She pattered towards me and thrust her muzzle between my hands because she was puzzled and needed comfort. She knew in her blood what I knew in my mind, that she would never run again – she was too old.

The sky remained blue and the picnickers fed and frolicked but we had heard something they had not – the first faint notes from on high calling Re'ach home, wherever that is for big black dogs.

In the meantime we trotted back to our earthly home, and I

said it with liver, a language she understood. We lived together contentedly for five years longer, and then she died peacefully in her sleep.

I remembered all this last week when I arrived back from Spain, tired but untroubled after a sleepless night in the departure lounge, for the loss of one night's sleep had never worried me before. But this time it did – my elastic had gone! My tiredness made me tip over teacups and the words I wrote didn't make sense. I thought of Re'ach and knew it was my turn to hear the first faint notes calling me home. I wandered into the chapel of Middlesex Hospital, and put my soul into God's hands, as she had put her head into mine.

And because I am a comfort eater like her, I sat in a nearby café and ordered not liver, but tuna rolls with raw onion, and custard pies.

Never had the custard seemed so smooth and creamy, nor the tuna so tasty. I found my phonecard and rang a friend – never had we felt so close. Life becomes lovelier when it has a frame. Those first faint notes, which had seemed so sad when I first heard them, begin to seem sweet. You can enjoy life when you don't own it and it doesn't own you.

Mink shmink!

I sulk over my supper because some of my savings have been 'corrected' on the stock exchange. 'Put not your trust in princes', says the Bible. Well, in future I won't. I'll put it in a building society instead.

My aunt tries to cheer me up, as she used to when I was a child.

'Knock, knock', she says brightly.

'Who's there?' I answer obediently.

'Arthur.'

'Arthur who?'

'O Lionel,' she whispers, 'I can't remember', and she passes a trembling hand over her face, the way elderly people do. I try to comfort her but she thrusts her post office savings book at me – 'It's yours dear', she says passionately. 'I'd give my right arm and leg for you.' I tell her, tactfully, I need neither.

My mother meanwhile has been poking about in a cupboard and pulls out a plastic bag. 'Here's your inheritance', she exclaims. My inheritance smells of moth balls – it's my mother's mink.

Nobody bought it for her, she says. She saved up for it herself

– penny by penny. She can't wear it now of course because she seems to have got smaller and the mink bigger, and she hasn't the strength to support it. Ma says it makes her look like Bond Street. But I don't care for fur, and it reminds me of *Watership Down*. My aunt looks at it wistfully and says, 'Mink Shmink!'

I thank my mother and go to bed. But before I can get to sleep, there's a tap at the door and my aunt peers in. 'I've remembered it, Lionel', she says proudly. 'Knock, knock.'

'Who's there?'

'Arthur.'

'Arthur who?'

'Ar-ther-mometer. Our thermometer', she adds in case I haven't got it.

I laugh, and my aunt goes out gratified.

I am just about to turn off the radio and try to go to sleep again when I sit up shocked. I hear about a bomb that has exploded in Ireland, and that innocent people have been murdered. Suddenly, I'm ashamed of my sulks and little losses and try to think of the real things in life. I remember Remembrance Day will soon be with us. I've a lot to remember.

Lying in bed I remember the families of those who died in Ireland and pray for them. I remember, for the first time in years, nice neighbours who were blown up in the Blitz. I remember dimly a boy I used to play with of my age. Why did he go, not me? I remember I'm the first generation in my family that hasn't had to fight in a world war. I remember how lucky I am I was born in Britain. I remember my mother's cousins who were not so lucky and got gassed in concentration camps – there were worse ways too!

Mink shmink!

What they would have given to be alive and enjoy my losses!
I hear my mother and aunt going to bed downstairs and
remember the real treasures of life, two elderly ladies who don't
hurt anyone and who love me to their last penny and pelt.

What the rabbi gave to the bishop

Many years ago I quarrelled with a friend, and it's taken me years to get over the grudge. But God moves in a mysterious way, and this is how He got me moving. It happened via a birthday, a bishop and a purloined lily. I can tell the story now, to my shame, because the principals in it are all dead except me.

I had arrived at a station on the Continent to attend a meeting of Jews, Christians and Muslims. The Christians in their nice Christian way thought that if we knew each other, we would love each other. Unfortunately the Jews wanted to know the Muslims, but the Muslims preferred to be matey with the Christians, and the Christians pursued the Jews, so that limited our progress.

But to get back to the lily. A breathless cleric at the station explained that it was the bishop's birthday and wafted me and a bemused Muslim to the bishop's palace. We stood in a long line of people greeting the bishop. They all bore presents. You know the sort of thing one gives – a second-hand Rembrandt, a medieval embroidered cope, a family heirloom or hot-house blossoms from your own greenhouse. And after they were presented, they were placed against a wall. Alone in the queue, my

Muslim colleague and I had nothing to offer – like two of the three wise men who had failed in their duty. It was embarrassing, and our cleric looked thoughtful. Suddenly he darted to the line of presents and came back with two lilies, lifted from one of the baskets near the wall. 'Give the bishop one each', he hissed. The Muslim looked grim holding his blossom, and I looked furtive holding mine. Both of us were built more like Oscar Wilde than the Blessed Damozel.

When we got to the bishop, our guide said fulsomely, 'Here is Rabbi Blue and he brings you a Jewish lily, and here is Mr So-and-So who brings you a Muslim lily!' I tried to get away quickly from the scene of the crime, but to my horror the bishop burst into tears and said he had never had a present like it – and this was quite untrue, because he had received the same lilies now twice over.

Reporters and photographers were summoned and they clicked away while I wondered if I would be discovered and end up as a terrible example in an anti-Semitic paper. My Muslim friend was trying, as well he might, to figure out if it was all a plot of the CIA or the KGB or MI5 or the Israelis, or all together in league with the lily-growers and Pre-Raphaelites.

But now for the grudge. I was just going back to the Continent for another conference. I sat in a synagogue trying to think about the meeting, but my mind kept drifting back to the bishop and the stolen lily. Well, I couldn't do anything about it now. Then my mind started rabbiting back to my grudge, to the friend I mentioned, and suddenly it dawned on me how God wanted me to tie them up. This time I would give that nice bishop, now dead, a real present. I would write a letter of apology to my friend and make him, the bishop, a present of a good deed done in his name. I did manage to write the letter – just – because I had promised it to the bishop in my prayers. Wherever the bishop now is, I hope he enjoys it as much as more normal gifts like talc, aftershave, Rembrandts, hankies, copes and chocolate. But these, as you will appreciate, may be inappropriate to his situation.

Now, you probably know what the actress said to the bishop. Well, if you don't by now, I certainly can't tell you – especially in a spiritual context. But now at least you know what the rabbi gave to the bishop. And as my old friend, who has now received the letter, said when I told him the story, 'The ways of God are kinda weird.' And that's quite enough tangled uplift for now.

My paranoid pooch

I sat on a park bench near the dog cemetery opposite Lancaster Gate station and thought about clever and classy dogs. Though the cemetery was firmly locked, I had peered through the railings and read fragments from the tombstones. It was a mausoleum of upper-crust canines, all of them noted when alive for their fidelity, integrity, intelligence and looks. They had the lot.

And I began to think of my poor pooch Re'ach, who had died not far away at the age of 18 and who had none of those qualities in any abundance. She was a big-boned bitch, a mongrel mixture of Labrador, Alsatian and other oddments. She was very large and rather loony, because she thought she was a lap dog but she wasn't built that way. Nor was she intelligent or ingenious or brave. If any burglar had the sense to bring along dog chocs, she was his – for the duration of the choc drops, that is.

She knew where the drops were kept, of course, in a plastic box with a lid, on top of her toys. But she never learned about lids. She just howled piteously beside it, until some weakling bribed her to stop.

She was also quite paranoid. If there was a bang from an exhaust, she was away like a rabbit, not a dog, seeking sanctuary under my bed, where she stayed until the end of hostilities. She was convinced until her dying day that 'they' were all gunning for her, Re'ach, as if they had nothing better to do with their time. (Did she learn it from me?)

She was no brave bonzo, as I have said. Despite her big body, she was girlish and terrified of mice, though the way she dealt with any particular mouse was novel, but ill-considered and quite mad. When she saw one, she poked her head into a cupboard, closing her eyes tight shut, so as not to see the very mild mouse, who seemed quite fond of her.

I have known many more intelligent dogs of far better character. I knew a lovely one in Malta called Honey. She was the only dog I've ever met who could smile – most dogs look clerically grave. But if you called out 'Honey', then she would curl back her lip and expose her molars in a fearsome grin. I had never seen a dog curl its lips before, and the result was unnerving but very clever.

The most intelligent dog I have ever met had only three legs. Someone must have kicked him as a puppy in a Mediterranean village. This had dislocated his hip and rheumatism had set in. His name was Mac and he lived among the garbage dumps. Though wary of humans, quite sensibly because they can be very nasty animals indeed, he was judicious about them. Selectively, with sense and discrimination, he made friends and acquaintances among them, though without illusion.

But to return to Re'ach, every part of the park reminded me of her. Once she tried to chase a duck, but the bird had turned and Re'ach had fled insanely across the green and jumped into my lap, all wet and sticky, reminding me with woofs and trembling that I was her protector.

Another time, while looking for some sunken stick, she spied a stockbroker type, pointing out with his polished stick a spire near Sloane Square. His smart gentleman's stick Re'ach quite wrongly regarded as her original stick, now sunk but miraculously renewed and restored. It was impossible to shake her conviction of ownership for she could only keep one idea at a time in her tiny but tenacious mind. There was a tussle, a tirade of blistering oaths and barks, and two black paw marks appeared on the stockbroker's fawn slacks. I tried to disarm Re'ach with the same intensity with which she tried to own the brolly. It did neither of us any good.

It's really a wonder she wasn't assassinated, but at 18 years old she died peacefully in Bayswater, near her beloved park, with her head in my lap. I didn't get her a memorial stone but I made a gift to an animal charity in her name. Perhaps 'charity redeems from death' works for dogs as well as for humans. I hope so, because heaven for me will always encompass an early autumn morning in a park with reddening leaves and bright blue sky, and a big black dog.

Our incomplete world

You wake up on a Monday morning, pick up the newspaper, switch on the radio, and wonder what sort of a world you're in. You've got your own personal problems – there's the tax form falling through the letter box and an awkward interview with your boss, and there's no marge left in the fridge. You feel gruff and growly already. And when you turn on the radio, you shoot bolt upright and whimper because there's been another plane disaster – this time on a route you've flown on many times – death is very close. You need a cup of tea fast.

Some people say God is everywhere and in everything, so evil doesn't really exist. It's just good in disguise. We can't see it, that's all. I once tried to see the world that way and it made me cross-eyed. Neither concentration camps nor plane disasters are good in disguise. Dead bodies, weeping relatives are never good.

Some people take the opposite line and say if hell exists, then this is it. But that doesn't fit the facts either.

I meet too much goodness and love in this world for that – too much charity, too much kindness.

I think things go wrong and disasters happen because the world is an incomplete sort of place. Like you and me, it's struggling towards its own perfection, but it hasn't got there. It's still going through its birth pangs.

So what's our place in it? Well I once sat in a church not far from a concentration camp, and thought about all the tragedies that had happened there. 'Why, God, didn't you take a hand in it?' I cried. Then I thought – how can God have hands? – He's pure spirit. But if He hasn't got hands, is He any use? Then it suddenly hit me. We're God's hands in the world and He works through us to complete His creation.

So don't dive back under your duvet as you read the news. Religion means facing facts, not fleeing from them. Get up quickly, have your cup of tea, and work out what you can do. Can you comfort someone on the plane, or give something to a disaster fund? Monday morning can be dreadful – that's true, but then that's why you're here. You might look and feel a mess, but you're God's representative – His hands on earth, working to complete His creation.

It's what we were created for. So let's get up, and get on with it.

Strewth!

'Lord,' I said this morning as I was shaving, 'what's all this about hell?'

For a moment He said nothing, but He's quite perceptive really, so He continued, casual like, 'Anything bothering you, Lionel? What's up?' And, of course, He was right. I was upset because I had got talking to a man who seemed so nice at first that I gave him a coin for his cause. He then explained to me that he wanted to warn me about hell. I'd heard that one before and smiled. But I couldn't stop his explanations. He was single-minded and serious, and step by ghastly step he demonstrated my danger to me.

I didn't follow it all, but somewhere in the cosmos there was a vast concentration camp. God was the commandant of this hell and His angels supplied the torturers and the gas. Unlike the Third Reich, it wouldn't last for a thousand years but for ever. I would go to it, he said, and all my family. My poor old mother and aunt hadn't endured enough in this world, apparently. God would have it in for them in the next as well.

I was annoyed with the man, and more annoyed with me, because he scared me stiff in spite of myself. Being a wobbler, I am always impressed by strong-minded people. And even if God forgives my sins, I never find it easy to forgive myself.

'Well, is there a hell?' I asked God apprehensively, waving my razor upwards.

'What did they teach you in the seminary?' He said.

'Well, the rabbis discussed it one and a half thousand years ago.'

'And what did they decide?' He seemed interested.

'They decided it didn't exist – but only by a majority vote.'

'Anything more?' He asked quite curiously.

'Some said, though they were in a minority, that we were already in hell. This world was it!'

'Well, some are certainly', He said sadly. 'Which reminds me, Lionel. Instead of worrying about hell so much, I want you to work at it a bit more. There's that poor old chap who says he's got AIDS. If you rang him up and did his shopping and went round for a natter and a cuppa, you might turn his hell into heaven this morning.'

'But I'm neurotic about catching things', I said. 'It might be heaven for him but it would be hell for me.'

'Don't be silly, of course it won't', said God. 'If you visit him, you know jolly well I'll visit you, and if I'm present, how can it be hell? Really?' He sounded rather miffed.

'Can I really change hell into heaven?' I said hastily, trying to be tactful and shift the conversation.

'I don't see why not', He answered mollified. 'After all, they're both inside you.'

'By the way,' He added hesitantly, 'forgive Me for asking,

Lionel, but why did your acquaintance say I created this cosmic concentration camp?'

'Out of love,' I said, deadpan, 'because You liked the inmates so much.'

'Strewth!' God said – a word I have never ever heard Him use, either before or since.

Real listening!

I tell a friend proudly that I have been asked to give a lecture on Empathy. 'Why you?' she says startled. 'You're a nice chap, Lionel, and mean well but you're one of the least empathetic people I know.' Now, she's not completely right because I have learned some lessons from Life, the great guru, over the years but she's not completely wrong either. I've got a lot of work ahead to become an empathetic listener, and I've left it late in the day because I'm 70-plus, but at least I have begun to realize what empathy means, or rather what empathetic listening means because that's the aspect of it which is most relevant to my life and my work.

I've learned a lot from a priest friend of mine who knocked two coal bunkers together in a swinging part of London and set up a listening post. Word got around that he would be in residence as the bars, dance halls, backrooms and clubs were closing to whoever dropped in and to whatever they wanted to talk about and they didn't even have to talk – they could just stay silent with him. He would just try to listen with all his attention, whether to their spoken language, their body language or their silence, and wouldn't counsel or advise unless asked to do so, and even then he preferred to help the caller advise her- or himself.

And all sorts of people did drop into his converted coal bunkers because London is very big and very lonely, and feels even lonelier when you have not found a partner for the night to keep you warm or keep you company.

Some who came to his listening post wanted to seduce him or rape him, some couldn't utter but their body language said it all and he and they just held hands which also says it all. Some wanted to mug him, kiss him or strip in front of him. But after the vaudeville was over, many stayed talking, crying or in silence while he gave them his attention, as he had promised with all his heart and mind.

Giving even ten minutes of one's attention to someone else is one of the most difficult things I know. At the seminary where I trained to be a rabbi, I was taught to talk fluently and wisely. Like any healthy youngster, I enjoyed hearing the sound of my own voice, so if you needed an impromptu sermon in a hurry, or a funny after-dinner speech, or a funeral oration, or a stand-in for a lecturer who hadn't shown up, I was your man.

But nobody taught me to listen. I was expected to pick that up en route. And I find it requires not just techniques but a deep change in me – a spiritual one. It means that the other person has to matter to me as much as I mean to myself.

Here are examples of what I mean.

At the beginning of my ministry, many decades ago I must emphasize, I used to cheat when doing my hospital visiting. (I didn't like hospitals because the sight and smell of blood made me nauseous.) Well, I entered a ward cheerily and said upbeat things to the patients in a firm confident voice. The patients looked interested in what this visitor from outer space who has erupted into their ward was up to. 'Why, you do look well, Mr So-and-so!' I exclaimed 'Why, you're beginning to look better already, Mrs X.' And Mr So-and-so and Mrs X stared back at me blankly and wearily, knowing that they weren't looking any better than yesterday. They also knew I wasn't saying all this garbage to help them, but to help me. I couldn't solve their problems or even cope with their having them. I could only say my party piece but I couldn't empathize, I couldn't listen and enter into their situation. So I took the easy way out.

It was the same with dying people. I tried to encourage them by telling them that the body has all sorts of powers of recuperation. I didn't mention the word death, though that was the subject in their minds and mine. I wanted to brighten them up and me up too, even if the good cheer I was peddling was based on avoidance. For this sort of bromide it was better if I did the talking and they just listened and didn't interrupt.

It was only later that I learned I didn't have to talk at all and I didn't have to have all the answers. Empathy was just letting their hand lie loosely in mine, so that they knew I was with them and they could drift away when they wanted. Once again I learned from my priest friend that my hand should not clutch them or seem to restrain them. Once again body language was truer than talking.

One last example which I've made up. Say a man comes to see me and says 'Rabbi, I've just knifed my dad.' He is naturally in a state of shock. While he continues talking, the following thoughts and questions race through my mind.

– Oedipus?

– Did I ever want to do that to my dad?

– Should I make him a cup of tea? Where's the sugar?

– Is it phantasy?

– Does he need therapy?

– What an interesting morning!

All these thoughts mean that I am not listening empathetically to him at all. I'm listening to my own solutions, my own thoughts, my own bromides, my own theology. I am certainly not giving him my attention. My own self-absorption is too strong. There may come a time for theology and solutions but much, much later when he has finished what he has to say and I've listened, really listened with my heart as well as my mind and chewed it over.

This lack of empathetic listening, or indeed any type of listening, is a great preoccupation of people now. It is a paradox that just as the means of communication such as mobiles, email, counsellors, therapists, Internet, social workers and analysts has increased, the amount and quality of true deep listening has contracted. Talking is a way we use to cover up the truth – not to communicate it or reveal it. It is the Tower of Babel problem.

I cannot, of course, quantify this assertion but here is an example of the popular jokes people tell each other. And remember jokes represent their real thoughts about their real lives. These jokes are especially critical of the caring professions to which I and many of you belong.

The young psychiatrist totters down to the hospital common room for his coffee break. He sits down at a table and watches his elderly colleague wolfing down smoked salmon sandwiches followed by cream éclairs. 'How can you eat so much after listening to all their piteous stories?' he bursts out.

'Who listens?' mumbles his elderly colleague, compulsively stuffing himself with even more comfort food.

And here's an example from my own life which is not a joke but true. In my late teens I realized beyond doubt that I was gay, the expression of which was a criminal offence in Britain before 1967. I needed advice urgently, being an only child with normal needs and having no brothers who could enlighten me. I went to see some ministers of religion. A rabbi ordered me out and the Christian ministers disappeared over the horizon fast as soon as I put my problem to them bluntly. My mother burst into tears and said it was all her fault, which didn't help her or me much, and a doctor took the easy way out and told us all not to worry because I was bound to grow out of it, which I didn't. In the end, by chance, I met an analyst at a party who asked me what I thought about it and how the world appeared to me, and actually listened to my reply. This was empathetic listening and it released the floodgates of my pent-up feelings. It was a new point of departure. I wasn't going round in circles any more.

Why is such empathetic listening so difficult for us? Probably because our parents, like most parents, never listened to us very much as children. They always knew better about how we felt than we knew ourselves. Since childhood experience goes very deep, most of us still do not understand what real listening is. This is a great handicap. So how do we set about learning it now that we ourselves are adults?

My best teachers have been my problems and failures in life. They are not empathy but have been my stepping stones towards it. A rabbi once said to me 'Mr Blue, your successes make you clever but only your failures make you wise.' And he was right. They are my spiritual capital. They are the only way I learn compassion, mercy and what it's like being at the wrong end of the stick. They point the way by which I can go beyond sympathy to the beginnings of empathy.

A lady stands outside a London supermarket. She is wearing cast-off clothes, and two plastic bags beside her contain all her possessions. A big city is full of such down-and-outs. At Oxford I had a bad breakdown and nearly became a drop-out too. It is marked on my memory. That is why I do not merely sympathize with her but can, after all those years, begin to empathize with her. It is something we share.

A young man asked me if I would help him with his CV. He was applying for jobs after university. Sure, I said, and then he told me the help he wanted. I was a smooth writer, he said, which I took as a compliment, and he wanted me to help him remove all his mistakes, failures and problems from the record and we should do it so smoothly that it would appear as if they had never happened. I told him to think again because anyone who presented me with such a smooth life would get no job from me. I repeated to him those words of my teachers that 'only your failures will make you wise'. My young man then told me I was not of this world and he would find someone else. I agreed with him that success and failure are dependent on the world you wish to enter. Failures and problems may do you no good in the rat-race world focused on success but they may be very relevant for you in the spiritual life, the beyond life which encloses it and which we experience even in this one.

What are the differences between sympathy and empathy? Well, the former is hierarchical, which is why most religious or ideological establishments prefer it. It implies someone on high who helps someone below. It is also quite self-conscious. Empathy is the fellow feeling which is so much part of us that we are scarcely conscious of it. It implies that we are both in the same boat and we listen and speak to each other out of fellow feeling. 'Hath not one father created us and are we not brethren to one another?'

Now, religious institutions, churches, synagogues, etc. do not like hearing their members out. For a variety of reasons, which include a desire to be helpful, avoidance and megalomania, they prefer to answer problems rather than listening to them. Like the parents in our childhood, they know more about how we fancy we feel than we do ourselves. Marxism was exactly like religion in this. Its adherents might be sympathetic but they were above you and knew what was better for you than you knew yourself, so why waste time listening?

You only have to look at most places of worship to realize that empathy is difficult because their hierarchical concepts are in their very structure. God lives in the Ark or on the altar. From on high he dribbles down a little bit of his truth to his ministers and wardens on the raised dais a little below him, and they in turn dribble a little of that on the hoi polloi at the bottom, provided of course they are good and deserving.

Perhaps this is why most of them are in a state of crisis now. Perhaps the crisis arises from the fact that at their best they are sympathetic institutions but not empathetic ones. They can give answers, but find it hard to listen and feel what they are listening to. They still have to learn another way of looking at the religious order. Perhaps God is not in the Ark at all but among us – in the congregation. Perhaps their answers do not fit our situation because they have never really felt what our situation is. Religious perception flows down but does not flow up. Perhaps the task of the Church is not to be so ready with answers at the present but instead to help us grow up and find our answers ourselves. Perhaps the sympathetic Church has to become the empathetic Church before we can all move on.

It is time. The official answers in our time have not been that good or even applicable, and their involvement in our world's problems has not always been for the best. It is no secret that religion does not just have the answer to problems; it is a big part of the problem itself. Religion does much good and for me personally it is welded into my life and experience. We only have to look at the political hot spots today to see this, whether in the Middle East, Far East, Ireland or Yugoslavia. Unfortunately the faith of big sections of it is expressed by shouting, fulminating and condemning rather than listening, especially empathetic listening. But the sheer amount of noise does not hide the insecurity and fear they try to cover.

I was told this story about Gertrude Stein when she was ill. I cannot vouch for it – it is only anecdotal – but it certainly fits what I know of her. While ill, she drifted back into a momentary consciousness. 'What's the answer?' she said puzzled, and then drifted back into unconsciousness again. Then she suddenly opened her eyes and remarked in a puzzled tone, 'But what's the question?' We could all learn from her, especially clerics and ecclesiastical bureaucrats like me.

Substitute for love

A lady wrote to me, asking if I could help her because her great love was ending. It was horrible, she said, like watching television and seeing all the colour drain out of it. Could religion help her?

Well, I'll try not to cheat and I'll be both religious and realistic, for though it's not easy to keep them together, it's a cop-out if you don't try. Yes, my dear, unless somebody else happens with indecent haste, the sadness is going to stay around for quite a while, and religion won't solve your loss, only help you to live with it.

But it's not fatal. People die of famine, not love — at least in all my years as a minister, I've only seen it happen to a dog, not a human being.

It's going to be tough living on your own. The same plates you didn't wash up in the morning will stare at you when you come back, and cooking for one isn't easy and at first you might burst into tears over your chop.

But there's still no need to take it that heavy, dear. A love affair isn't the purpose of your life on earth, and sex isn't all that it's cracked up to be. It's often just a sideshow.

After all, falling in love wasn't as nice as you were led to expect, and falling out of it has its compensations. Think of all the advantages. You can tot them up:

You'll have time to see your old friends again.

You won't have to hold your tummy in.

Your telephone bill will go down.

You can push away the cottage cheese and low-fat yoghurt and treat yourself to a slice of Black Forest gateau instead.

You can go to bed at a reasonable hour with a cup of cocoa, and who cares if the cocoa trickles over your cold cream.

You can fall asleep to Radio 3 playing more baroque chewing gum and not to a snorer's Ninth Symphony.

You'll be less nervous, so won't break so much china.

And though sadder, you will be safer, for it's not prudent to hand so much power over yourself to another human being – only to God.

And also it isn't necessary. You don't need someone else to tell you you're worthwhile and lovable. You can do that yourself.

You don't need somebody else to find peace. The quietness is already inside you, if you decide to use it. How long is it since you sat back and prayed for it and not just presented God with a shopping list as if He were a department store?

Through prayer you might even begin to discover the seed of your next love in the death of the old. Your second affair might be with love itself. And that is a very deep truth, though it comes from a juke box.

Ah, you will say, but if there's no person, what about sex? You can't have sex with love itself. Yes, it is difficult loving without sex if you are used to sex regularly. But, being realistic, not romantic, some sex is just habit, some of it is in your mind, not your body, and a lot of it isn't all it's cracked up to be. Sublimation isn't a dirty word. For example, I've been working so hard lately on cookery books, I haven't even had time to have a depression, and you can apply that to your sex life too.

Prayer and Black Forest gateau don't make for ecstasy at first, but in combination they can make you content, and if you've been let down in love, some quiet contentment is a great relief.

The old Jewish people I knew only aspired to contentment, for their lives were hard. If they were at death's door, the kind Irish nurses at the London Hospital used to ask, 'Are you comfortable now, Mr Cohen?' and because they couldn't understand much English, and who had ever worried about their comfort, they were puzzled and said, 'No need to worry, nurse! I get a living. I get by!'

Loss of status

She had silky brown hair, and long lashes framed her liquid brown eyes. These she half closed as she gazed at me with a sideways glance. The convent buildings slept in the heat haze behind the trees. We were alone.

As I came closer, she suddenly pressed herself against me. We lay side by side in the grass, and I fed her cow parsley. Occasionally she butted me in the belly to express her feelings.

It was Emily, the convent goat, who had taken a shine to me, and when they came to lead her back to her pen, she again half turned to give me one last lingering look.

To be the recipient of love is a wonderful thing, and that night I lay awake fantasizing. She could bed down in my garden shed. I would feed her cow parsley and she would feed me her yoghurt and reduce my milk bills – an arrangement both reasonable and Franciscan.

Next morning before breakfast, I rushed to her meadow and halted in shock. She had changed into a very nasty goat, unlike the loving animal of yesterday. She stood on a hillock braying boastfully, and butting the other nannies. She gazed at me briefly, bared her teeth and brayed again in triumph.

At breakfast the nice nun who attended to the goats and the

guests saw that I was hurt. 'Don't judge her harshly,' she said, 'that goat has suffered.' Her sad story turned my anger into pity. Emily was a brown goat in a herd of white ones who never accepted her. And having no kids, she had lost all status in her herd, which obsessed her.

Cleverly, under the guise of love, she had manipulated my attention, because the attention of any human being gave her the status she craved and schemed for. Now having got it, she had no more use for me. Like many modern people, she rejected the real things of life for their shadow. I said farewell to the kind nun and returned home. My letterbox was so jammed with junk mail, I could scarcely open the door. A coloured credit card would make me the envy of other borrowers. An exclusive travel ticket would entitle me to use a lounge and loo only sat on by better-class bottoms. A club announced it was exclusive to executives.

'Enjoy the goodies but beware the poison bait!' I said to myself. Enjoy the good opinions of others, but don't let your self-respect depend on them. Remember poor Emily who sacrificed true love for status, the substance of things for their shadow. It's a pity she couldn't chew her way out of the garden into the chapel, to meditate on the time when God will sort out His sheep from the goats. For, when all we creatures pass before Him, He will gaze into our substance, not our status in the herd. Such knowledge now would serve us well in the life of the world to come – and it would give us better balance in this world too.

Now you may know the stories of 'A Man Called Horse' and 'A Fish Called Wanda'. Well, here's the sad story of 'A Goat Called Emily'. Ponder it well!

Is God snoozing?

In the morning paper there was another spate of letters and articles all about God. Some of the writers said He was dead, some said He was alive, but lived only in them. Some said He was dead but She was alive. One correspondent implied He was asleep or snoozing, though he didn't put it that way, and another thought he could analyse Him, given the right cosmic couch, of course. He suspected incipient megalomania.

But everybody joined together in a general mope about religion. It was going down, it was going to bits or to the bad in a big way. Ministers were moping, rabbis were recriminating, and bishops were bumbling over its fate. 'Look at the churches,' they said, 'look at the congregations – tiny! Look at the collection plates – pitiful! Not even enough to give the parson one portion of plaice with two of chips, let alone prop up the church tower.' They wagged their heads woefully.

Well, some of it is true, of course. Lots of congregations are declining because, to be honest, they are constipated. It's an odd word to use but quite accurate. You go in, you take part in the ceremonies and say the right words. You sit down, stand up, change hymn books, and sit down again. You kneel, bow, prostrate and otherwise contort. You put your prayer book in, you put your prayer book out, you wave your hymn book in the air, and you shake it all about, but . . . nothing has happened. You aren't any holier or wiser. Was your religious hokey-cokey really necessary? Apparently not – the collection plate says so – why give something for nothing?

But just because some forms of formal religion are dead or dying, this doesn't mean religion has had it. Perhaps everybody is just looking in the wrong place, that's all. You don't have to go to synagogues or cathedrals for religious experiences or ecstasies – in fact you had better not, for they would not be welcome. They might upset the sermon or the choir, and you would be asked to leave.

Quite a few people find divine grace in London supermarkets, which are not planned for purveying such products. A lady on a park bench told me how she was lining up at the checkout, a man was pushing her in the rump with his trolley, and the woman in front was fiddling with her cheque book and credit card and was holding up the entire queue, who were snapping at her, at the harassed girl behind the till and at each other.

Then suddenly, for her, the whole situation turned inside out (that is how she described it), and she felt giggly about the next jab in her rump and experienced a wave of compassion for the poor person on the till. She offered a pen which worked to the lady with the cheque book, and waggled her behind invitingly to present a good target for the trolley of the mighty macho male behind her. It was a giggle, and she was overcome with compassion and love for everybody there. She not only loved them, she liked them, which is much harder.

What did I think of it? she asked. It was a real religious

experience, I told her, as genuine as any you find in tracts or in scriptures. But in a supermarket? she said. Well, the spirit bloweth where it listeth – it says so in all the best scriptures and why should we be more choosey than the spirit?

And though people are not swarming into formal services, a lot of people pop in for a little prayer when no one is looking or keeping statistics. At breakfast time, in a little place of worship in a West End side street, there were two or three cleaners, a roadsweeper, some tourists from Park Lane hotels, some secretaries and stockbroker types, a beggar or two snoozing, and me.

I have to repeat that God was alive and well and awake when I met Him last, but He seems to keep odd hours.

Senile delinquent

On the crowded bus I offered my seat to a senior citizen. 'Keep it yourself, Grandad', he said nastily. He then wriggled as far down the bus as he could get while the rest of the passengers tittered. Occasionally he threw me a malevolent look. Because your world grows old with you, you notice the passing of time in strangers but not in yourself or your friends.

But time had passed, and I was reminded of it when I rang up to make enquiries about sheltered accommodation for an elderly friend. 'How old is he?' said the lady at the other end. 'Over eighty, but very fit', I replied. 'Oh dear,' she said, 'that's far too late. You have to come into the scheme much earlier.' 'What, seventy?' I asked. 'Well,' she answered apologetically, 'perhaps a little earlier than that.' 'Sixty?' I said stiffly. 'Yes,' she said, 'that would be about right, but don't leave it too late.' 'You mean,' I said icily, 'I should not be applying for my friend but for myself.' 'How old are you?' she asked briskly. 'Fifty-seven', I replied sulkily. 'Just right!' she said, 'I'll send you a form', and she rang off hurriedly.

It rankled! So I signed on for a holiday where I could learn to be my age and snooze with fellow seniles. But it wasn't like that. Our hotel and hostesses were lovely. Nothing was too much trouble, whether it was TV, tea, or transport by air, coach or camel. One day we had culture in chilly churches and on the next we trotted in a conga line through a casbah, where we feasted on a combination of herb tea and couscous with a belly dancer who wore combinations, of the woolly sort I thought, and a fender round her front like a jeep.

At lunch and dinner we were given our bottles, like the ones we had as babies, but with stronger stuff inside, of course – no teats but with the same effect. They certainly sedated me into a stupor and after lunch I dozed with drooping jaw in the hotel lounge. I once wondered what rubbish roams through the mind of old people, marooned between meals. Now I know!

Pain from the past flooded my mind as helplessly I relived a passion of long ago. It had started with the usual high hopes and ended with the usual rows and recriminations. Frantically I added up the pluses and minuses to my ego – the hits I'd scored and the hurts I'd endured.

'Must it end like that?' I cried out in my sleep (perhaps someone saw my lips move).

'Not necessarily', said a familiar voice within me.

'But I can't change what's gone', I said.

'You can always alter the ending', said the voice. 'You're alive so the story hasn't stopped. Try and see it again through my eyes.'

I forced myself to try, because if I didn't do a repair job on the past, it would poison my present and my retirement. All the sums I totted up began to seem so silly. Even if you lose someone you've loved, a bit of them has become part of you, and when you think you hurt them, you're the one who screams. This means that you've got to forgive if you want to be forgiven, because they are only two sides of the same coin. I no longer knew any name or address where I could find forgiveness, but I'd make it up and do a good turn to someone else instead.

'Charity always cheers up a sad story', said my uninvited voice.

'I won't behave like that next time', I promised.

'Aren't you too far gone for a next time?' said the voice with amusement.

'With God all things are possible', I answered sweetly.

'Hmmm . . .' said the voice and abruptly changed the subject. 'Look, Lionel, there's a time for penance and a time for pastries.'

Sure enough, a hubbub filled the lounge and I woke up. There was tea on the house for all and we got three biscuits each.

A piece of potato

Not long ago, I got a piece of potato lodged in my eye (no, I do not know how it got there!). The eye was bandaged and blinkered, and I walked round London, bumping into street furniture and saying 'Pardon'.

My appearance became even more piteous when I slipped on a piece of fried fish, although I only wanted chips, and got a knock on the knee. This resulted in my being issued with a stick. Together with my bandaged eye it made me a spectacle and a conversation piece, as fellow Londoners took it for granted I must be hard of hearing as well – although their logic still escapes me.

On the whole, people were very nice to me. I was given precedence in Harrods' sale and a lady stood up for me in a train. I was fed with buns by a troop of foreign boy-scouts as their daily good deed. The buns were fresh, and I felt like a bear, though much happier than the bored ones in the zoo.

An American lady from a Park Lane hotel helped me across a road I did not want to cross, but she was interesting and amiable and I liked being led, though it took me a long time to get back to the place where I'd started and I had to wait until she stopped looking back to check on me.

I seemed to raise enormous feelings of guilt wherever I appeared. Nobody knew how to cope with me on the crowded bus. As I stood in the gangway, a contented young couple got into a heated argument – their first perhaps – and it was over me.

'That poor doddery old thing', said the girl. 'Why don't you get up, dear, and let him rest?'

I resented her adjectives but to get a seat I was prepared to swallow my pride, so I quivered very slightly to support her words.

Her companion was made of sterner stuff and, glueing himself beside her, whispered urgently in her ear. I could not hear his words but I could reconstruct them from her reply. 'Oh,' she said doubtfully, 'it's healthier for him if he's upright – it's better for his bottom.' She blushed prettily as she delicately repeated his words.

I quivered again, anxious to see who would win this cosmic struggle between good and evil.

'And also,' added the young man, sensing his advantage, 'if I got up you would have to sit next to him, wouldn't you, and you don't know where he's been.'

'Well then, perhaps you're right about his . . . posture', she said, weakening. 'I wonder if he's clean.'

'Can't be,' her swain said reassuringly, 'grubby as a goat', and he gave her another hug.

With a sensuous sigh his girl gave up and said, 'You're probably right, dear, you always are. . . .' The bus stopped abruptly in the West End and I was decanted, indignant at all I'd endured.

It was quite funny really. After all, I was not seriously hurt.

They prised the vegetable away from my eyeball and for a while I ate Chinese take-away, not fish and chips. I got attached to my stick and had to be shamed into giving it up. I hooked groceries on it and it did good service in queues. I also used it on door knockers, but then I thought what it was like really to be disabled in London and have to get about. People are nice but they're not consistent – they just can't keep up their generosity when they're pressed and, if you are disabled, that's hard.

The cost of coffins

I was chatting with an elderly nun I know about the cost of coffins. It was really rather grim, she said, how everything was going up, and it was very inconvenient. She had slept in a coffin for years, a modest one, though specially made for her, and though she could not say her coffin was comfortable or cosy – indeed it was not meant to be – she had to admit it fitted her well enough both physically and spiritually, and was really quite snug.

But to her surprise she had outworn her coffin, and as it had to be custom-built on the Continent, for the shoulders had to fit, a replacement was out of the question. A new one was dearer than a repro four-poster fitted with concealed amplifiers. Her mother superior had exclaimed that because of holy poverty this was out. It was too expensive and they would all have to resign themselves to comfort on a divan base like everyone else – if you could buy them without mattresses.

I sympathized with her on the loss of her coffin, because in a similar way I had become very attached to a shroud which I took with me on all my travels, and had recently mislaid. I had put it for safe keeping in a plastic bag and left it behind on a bar stool in Frankfurt Airport, so I cannot speculate on its fate.

It was a natty number in white cotton which my aunt ran up for me as a wedding present when I was wobbling towards matrimony. It had a festive look for she had sewn folds of artificial lace round the neck and cuffs. Even when I wobbled in the other direction, and had to send back most of the wedding presents, I kept my shroud – it was not the sort of thing you could 'return to sender'.

Like many Jewish people, I wear a shroud on some important festivals, such as the Day of Atonement, and eventually I hope to be buried in one. From the point of view of fashion, a shroud is not a success. I shall meet my maker looking like a piece of meat, a chop adorned with white frills, the kind you see in high-class butcher shops. A colleague told me brusquely that Aunty's shroud made me look like Gilda in *Rigoletto*, when she is fleeing from the Duke in a white nightie.

But its whiteness still recalls the purity from which I came and to which I shall return. Like Sister's coffin, it tells me that to enjoy the life of this world I should not clutch at it, for the world is not as solid as it looks, just as my shroud is not as silly as it seems. In fact, neither coffin nor shroud is ornamental but fundamental – because they can help you to live truly. If you know, for example, that an eternity awaits you, you stop being so greedy and can afford to enjoy the taste of the world a little more, for it is very like chocolate. If you suck it slowly, you get the flavour – if you gobble it, you just get indigestion.

This greed comes from insecurity and a feeling that the world will cheat you, which it must do if it is the only world and you treat it in this way. Only a sign of mortality can give you enough perspective on life to enjoy it. Some friends of mine leave a little corner of their living room unplastered, to remember that though their detached house is cosy with central heating, it is not their eternal home. Such knowledge prevents much pain.

But perhaps you're reading this at breakfast, propped against the teapot. 'Why, Fred,' I can hear you say, 'that rabbi's rabbiting on about coffins. It does make me feel queasy and queer so early in the morning. I should have read the newspaper instead. Pass me another kipper, dear, and that napkin. Yes, Fred, that one with the lace edging, just like the rabbi's. . . . Oh dear!'

Meeting the horizon

*This lecture was given at Canterbury Cathedral and then
served as Introductory Reflections to* 'Beyond Life',
Theological and Philosophical Reflections on Life after
Death, *edited by Dan Cohn-Sherbok and Christopher Lewis,
and published by Macmillan. My thoughts on this matter
have continued since I first gave that lecture so I have
extended it. Like Sigmund Freud, I think you need to know
how to die in order to know how to live.*

I felt disoriented. I had gone to visit an old-age home, when I
realized that the people I was visiting assumed from my dishevelled appearance that I had come to vet the place to find out
how quickly I could become an inmate, a resident like them.
Getting in wasn't that easy! I told myself tragically that I was
on the downward path to death. And this was true. But this is
the same for you, young as well as old. That's life!

But being religious and being Jewish, I was a laconic opti-
mist. So I sat for a long time over a cup of coffee considering
the situation, spying out the unknown territory that lay ahead
of me. There are lots of counsellors and guides who help
youngsters bridge the difficult gap between late adolescence

and early adulthood but few who will accompany you through the equally difficult time which leads from late middle age into old age. I see the oldies in my neighbourhood who are in it. They are soldiering on but not very happily.

The caring society is a hope and a dream, much of which has not yet materialized. Many oldies feel keenly the loss of independence, their varied treatment in geriatric wards – some wonderful, some contemptuous – and the loneliness of it all, especially if they've no family or they're the lone survivors.

But then I bounced back. I had my assets. I had a pension (depleted but basic), a free travel pass to ride the buses, a senior railcard and lots of freebies and reductions if I could winkle them out. More seriously I had my life experience, lots of it, of real but indeterminate value, also my spirituality and religion ditto. I also had a partner and I actually enjoyed love more than I did as an adolescent because now it was an option, not a compulsion.

So I decided not to be a foolish virgin with no thought of the morrow, but learn how to cope with problems I couldn't solve, such as my mortality. In my experience, whenever I had faced such situation honestly and invoked my inner Friend for help, something had happened. My problems had turned inside out, some minuses had become plusses and some horrors had even turned into humour.

My first thought was about the afterlife and this crumbled as soon as I mentally touched it, for when I die, time and space will die with me and neither before nor after will exist. And there lies another problem: all one can ever know is life, whether this life, another sort of life or eternal life. So death can never be experienced. But although you cannot speak of an

after-life, you can talk about a beyond-life. And that is something which I, and lots of people, have come to, not through
dogma or official teaching, but by experience. It is a reasonable
way to approach religious matters. After all, it is 'taste and see
that the Lord is good' in the Hebrew Scriptures, and 'by their
fruits ye shall know them' in the Gospels. So the proof of the
pudding really is in the eating. One should not puff one's
goods in religion. One should remember that honest descrip-
tions apply to religious metaphysics as much as they do to
goods in the supermarket. Our experiences do not prove what
you might call a 'beyond-life' but they do point to it. And if
you are prepared to base your life on it, then it does not let you
down. Now, what are these experiences? Well, there are a number of very general experiences which I have and lots of other
people have too.

The first thing is that a lot of people have out-of-the-body
experiences of some type or other. For me it usually occurs not
in churches or synagogues but at receptions, committee meetings and during rows, etc. While I am doing the expected
things, a part of me feels as if it had stepped out of me and
looks down on all of us, with pity and compassion for myself
and everybody else. Lots of other people recognize this too.

There is another experience which many people share, and
that is the feeling or the intuition (or whatever you like to call
it) that although the world is not a bad place, and one can
enjoy it to an extent, at the same time it is not home. This
thought or feeling comes upon me in this situation: I am dark-
looking and when I went on one of my package holidays, I was
in the luggage checkout at Palma Airport, and some German
tourists rushed up to me, thinking that I was Spanish, and

started to speak to me in bad Spanish. I replied in equally bad German and I had to tell them, 'Entschuldigen, aber . . .' ('Excuse me but I'm a tourist too.'). And it suddenly occurred to me as I said it that this does not just apply to that situation – it applies to lots of other situations in life. I *do not* feel that this is home. I am just a sojourner here, as the scriptures say, and lots of human beings feel like that. Yes, this world is an interesting place – yes, you strike up friendships in the departure lounge – but sooner or later your flight is called and off you go. You are a bit apprehensive about where you are going to, but at the same time this is not really the place where you belong and if you try to feel too permanent here, it always lets you down. It is not that sort of place. So that is another experience which I think that people have.

Another experience occurs when people go into a silent synagogue/church/place of worship. They often feel that they have stepped into a different dimension. In the stillness, they are not quite sure what is up, but they feel that they have stepped into another world. It can also be triggered by great art or music, or sometimes by love. Then you may find something interesting: that you can make that beyond-world happen. You do not just have to *wait* for it to happen; you can *make* it happen. Sometimes if you give yourself to it, and you can try this yourself, then the feeling comes back. You do something generous which is a bit dotty and a bit altruistic (you could kick yourself) but at the same time you get a kind of glow and you feel as if you have experienced the *gravity* of some unseen beyond-world.

Let me give you another example: I am in a train, reading a book on religion, which I am thoroughly enjoying, and I really am getting a great deal of benefit from it. But there is this lady standing up (a foolish virgin who has not reserved a seat). I try to ignore her but my book keeps on telling me, 'You jolly well stand up for her'. So finally, in a very grumpy fashion, I do, because I know that if I do *not* then I cannot carry on reading the book and getting the nice sensations from it. So I stand up, though part of me says 'You are a bloody fool', but another part of me feels that I have made that other world happen. And I think lots of people also feel as if they are pulled by a kind of gravity from some unseen world, which pulls their lives out of their normal trajectory and makes them do silly things, altruistic things, all sorts of odd things. But when they do them, once again that feeling returns.

You provide your own evidence and I think the real evidence for the beyond-life is not even in these experiences I have mentioned. I think the only evidence for it, convincing evidence, is the evidence you provide yourself. In other words, you have to *become* your evidence. You can talk glibly about the beyond-life, for and against, until the cows come home, but only when you invoke it and allow it to work on you and you see what it makes of you, only then is it convincing. It is only when, as it were, things turn inside out, that you find yourself not using it, but *it* using *you*. At the beginning this beyond-life is fun. It gives you little shivers down your spine, it gives colour to a rather drab life, it makes you have little chats with the cosmos, it makes you feel quite somebody. And you can play about with it quite a lot. But then there comes a point when it starts answering back, when it starts making demands on you. Then you are in a quandary because you either say 'Get out of my life' or 'Well, it was nothing really in the first place', in which case you have lost it and there is a real sense of grieving and bereavement if you do (I personally could not do that). Or else you have to go along with it, at least in part, and when you do that, you realize that something which started off as a nice idea packs a very powerful punch. And that is when you start sitting back and respecting it.

I think many people find that if you invoke that beyond-life, that other dimension, it has a great power. For example, alcoholics, who are not officially religious, say 'We rely upon a power greater than ourselves to help us out of our addiction'. They have found by experience that they cannot do without it. They do not call it God, they just say 'a power greater than ourselves'. Well, it affects anybody who really invokes it, and does not just play around with it – anybody who cries that most basic prayer, 'Help!' (because you are out of your depth), and you do find that something happens.

My parents wanted me to be a doctor but I could not because I cannot stand the sight of blood and so I faint. Whenever I have tried to give blood, I have always fainted and they have told me to go away because my blood is not worth the trouble it takes to get it. That is one reason why I became a rabbi: because souls are much less messy and gory than bodies. But life has a habit of turning back and biting you and I found myself visiting hospitals and that is becoming an increasing part of my work. Now when I start to go into hospital, I am not quite sure what is going to happen (am I going to faint because there is a lot of gore about?) – that is when I invoke that beyond-life. It gets me through my hospital visit. I can have my attack of nausea after I come out of the hospital (I can also have a cappuccino and a custard pie when I come out!) but it helps me over the stile while I am there. I think lots of people have found that.

I have found that beyond-life has also been important in my own personal life. I was living with someone for years – and then it finished. It was on the Continent. I knew it was ending. I remember going into a church and thinking 'What the hell do I do now?' I remember that, as if in a conversation, something was saying to me that all the loves I had in this life were reflections of the real thing and one day, but not in this life (perhaps at the end of it), I would meet the real thing. At least, that is how it came to me. I pushed the thought aside; it seemed too sentimental to bother about. But I remember that when we were back in London, trying to work out who owned what and we got to the business of 'I said', 'you said', 'he said', 'she said' (you know all the quarrels which go on with this sort of thing) and we were just about to have a real ding-dong of a row, of the kind that happen when couples break up, when I suddenly felt as if the face I was looking at, my friend's face, was a kind of mask and beyond it was this beyond-life. One moment the beyond-life was there, and the next it was not, as if a light was being turned on and off inside my friend's face. It was a funny sensation – I burst into laughter and said, 'Look, we can't carry on like this: let's go to the pub.' As a result, we ended things pleasantly and we still see each other. So, that beyond-life has also affected my personal relationships.

Sometimes this dimension has a personal face and some-times it has no face. At different times in one's life one adds more imagination or less imagination to it. People are aware that beyond the world of things there is another reality. You cannot deal properly with the world of things without relying upon that *other* reality.

I think the difficulty about the beyond-life is very simple – it is just not visible. But even people who just concern themselves with the world of visible things know very well that you cannot deal with the world of visible things justly or fairly or even constructively, without recourse to that *invisible* world. My thinking came to a head when I got my dog. Whenever I went out of the house, I died to her and when I came back *into* the house, she experienced it as a resurrection. This accounted for her rather rocky emotional life.

Now, we are the first animals in the evolutionary life who can give reality to things which are outside our senses. Our hold on that reality is very, very slight. It is a great fight, on our part, to be able to take that step and, as it were, improve on our animal heritage. We are, I think, the first of the animals who have ever got that far.

Why do people bother to invoke this other world at all, or try to become acquainted with it, become friends with it? I think it is because sooner or later the world of sensed things lets you down. It must do. Because everything that we are ever given in life sooner or later has to be given up or given away, which you can either do gracefully or with groans, grunts and passing the buck. But sooner or later the world of things *does* let us down, through illness, through somebody snitching somebody we love, through someone repossessing our home. And even if none of these things has happened, one day we are going to die.

Then, when that world of things lets us down, we try to get new strength and we suddenly invoke that world which is *not* sense. If it *is* invoked, as I have said before, something happens. Sometimes the world of things lets one down, either dramatically and catastrophically, as in a concentration camp or, sometimes, it is only saying goodbye to everybody, and dying quietly and gently and pleasantly. But it comes to the same thing. Then one has to put one's faith in that other dimension. Now, you can give that beyond-life a human face or not. Some of the greatest Christian saints, such as Teresa of Avila or John of the Cross, sometimes thought of that dimension as having a human face: the face of Christ. At the same time they also felt that sometimes it did *not* have that face; it was beyond any face. And I think that is a matter of temperament, environment and imagination: the clothes that you dress it in. But the reality of it is well-attested. It even works on a very practical level: you are wanting to go on holiday and you are looking at the holiday brochure and you check up – balcony? yes; sea view? yes; bath facilities?; three course meals twice a day? And that is fine. But then you know very well you can have all these things and it still does not add up to what you want. You can be happy and unhappy with or without them.

You see, the world of things deals with the comfort problem, but the happiness problem is something else, and that is something which comes from that beyond-life. It means peace with oneself, and coming to terms with one's anger. Comfort and happiness are not the same. And for happiness you have to deal with that beyond-life. Even agnostics and atheists have learned this. Marcus Aurelius, who was no friend to Christians, says that if god exists, then you should follow him; but if he doesn't, be like god yourself. He says that we should, as it were, construct a temple inside ourselves and go into that. That is fair enough. Whether you contemplate the absolute, have a love affair with Jesus, listen to the voice in the burning bush, it is the same kind of thing. People know, just from the business of going on holiday, that the problems of this world cannot be solved in its own terms. You have to invoke another dimension, for even this world to work. Otherwise you end up very disappointed and very annoyed.

Also, in practice, it's not easy defining where you end and other people begin, or where the living end and the dead begin. If you wish, you can make room inside your mind for someone whom you want to continue living in it. All sorts of people can inhabit your mind if you are prepared to give them houseroom. I find that, when I think of my own personality, it is not just tricks of speech that have been adopted from other people (odd expressions, etc.) but occasionally when I come to a situation, I know I can't do a certain action, sensible though it seems. Why? Because a girl I knew who has died still says in me, 'Lionel, how can you *possibly?*' and I know I cannot. I think also that religious people incarnate what they worship. So you can see Jesus or the Risen Christ, as it were, in the Christians who are devoted to him. That is, I think, the way that most people perceive somebody else's god. This sharp division as to where one person ends and another being begins is not firmly there.

Lately, this business of the 'near-death experiences' has come up. I do not know what to make of them – these circles of light and meeting people one knew. But one would also have to remember that one would have to meet the people one did not like, as well as the ones that one did. It might all be because of the lack of oxygen to the brain. Who can say?

Most people I have met, who have died, died puzzled because life is such an unfinished business and most people seem to die with the questions 'Why me? Why now?' At the same time, I have also noticed that when people accept that they are dying, a change happens. The problem comes in letting go. But once you have let go, people often give up their sleeping tablets and pain killers. Any nurse or doctor can tell you that. Once you look at where you are going to rather than where you have come from, then it is as if something in you relaxes and loosens up. Quite often you find, for example, at a deathbed that the dying person is really having to cope with and in an unexpected way comfort the people around him or her, not vice versa.

A rabbinic story has helped me: there is a strange text which says 'the day of one's death is better than the day of one's birth'. The rabbis asked 'How could this be?' And they said: 'At a birth, as the baby is born, everybody there thinks it is a wonderful thing, a matter of rejoicing. Everybody except one: the baby. The baby, which comes from the security of its mother's womb, to the cold world outside, has not experienced it as a birth. It has experienced it as a death. When we come to our death, it is the same situation but in reverse. The mourners see the world that the dead person is leaving and see it as a death, but the person who is dying may well be seeing the world he or she is going into and may experience it as a birth. Once again, the difference is your point of view.'

I used to go to dying people in hospitals, in cancer wards, or in AIDS wards, thinking 'I must do it but it is going to be dreadful'. The strange thing is that it is not dreadful. It is rather the opposite. I am not the only person who has felt this, because I have discussed it with other chaplains. Many of us feel that it is in these wards that we get our spirituality, that people seem to rise to the occasion of their death. It is as if part of them has already joined that beyond-life and a kind of peace comes from them. Also, the fact of death and dying in a ward does not bring on the horrors. On the contrary, it usually brings out a great deal of affection and love, and kindness. It was after coming from an AIDS ward that I suddenly realized that heaven is a place where people love each other, and hell is a place where they hurt and hinder each other. This AIDS ward was one of the closest to heaven I had known. There was a great deal of hugging and cuddling; they really were helping each other and I came away feeling elated.

I find that I need my own input of spiritual experience. If you are a professionally religious person, earning your living by it, you cannot just keep on giving. You need to get something. Where do you get it from? I get it from people in trouble. I get it from alcoholics, from dying people and from AIDS sufferers. These are the people who give me my spirituality. When I do retreats with them, their retreats start off where other kinds of retreats end, and we deal with the nitty gritty straight away. For them the beyond-life is not an idea, is not something they can debate. The whole of the material world is no longer substantial enough to lean on, therefore every resource has to come from that beyond-life, from that world which is not sense. Therefore the most unlikely people are forced to invoke it, or come to terms with it. When they do, an enormous flowering takes place and although I am supposed to *take* the retreats, in fact I get more out of them than I give. That is not banality or politeness, it is the truth. Many other people who do this work have experienced exactly the same sort of thing. When you are out of your depth and the ground seems to go away from under you, that is the time when you cry 'help'. You cannot get a sure footing on *this* life any more, so you call on that beyond-life in desperation, to help you, and the fact is that if you really do it with all your being, it supports you.

This is why, although I cannot talk about the after-life, I can talk about the beyond-life. I cannot prove it and it is not even good to, because all of us are secret materialists, who would love the things of the spirit to become material. This is why we would like holy statues to wink or to dance, and would like extraordinary miracles to take place. We would like to materialize the spirit, because we are materialistic. I cannot say I believe in the beyond-life. What I would say is that if you base your life on the beyond-life and its existence and invoke it, it just does not let you down.

The beyond-life has become more important to me as I've grown older. Looking back it seems to me that the first part of my life was led by the needs of my body, my struggle for survival and my coping or inability to cope with the bodily changes of puberty. This was followed by the years in which my mind led the way. I had to earn a living, prove myself and be successful in a competitive society. It was the time for acquiring things. But now when my body is crumbling and my memory fading, it is the time for my soul. The horizon of life is coming nearer and only my soul can lead me to it and through it . . . Now is the time for a very specialized form of giving – giving up! I should like to do it with good grace, and cheerfully.

My gypsyish mother managed it rather well. In one of the last conversations I remember having with her she said, 'Lionel, what you've done, you've done, but the rest is gravy.' How charitable! How encouraging! Good on yer, ma!